1'	2'	3'	5'	Page		1'	2'	3'	5'	Page
Fog	x		x		53	Corporate Stock	x		x		63
Health-Care						Contracts			x	x	64
Employment	x		x		53	Computer Benefits	x		x		65
Money			x	x	54	Business Planning			x	x	66
Stereo Systems	x		x		55	Sole Proprietorship	x		x		67
Auto Insurance	x		x		55	Establishing Credit			x	x	68
A Sense of Humor			x	x	56	Social Security System	x		x		69
U.S. Money	x		x		57	Limitations of our Earth			x	x	70
Learning to Read			x	x	58	Highway Funding	x		x		71
Inflation	x		x		59	CPA Examination			x	x	72
Employment			x	x	60	Emotions	x		x		73
Office Automation	x		x		61	Weather			x	x	74
Good Office Procedures			x	x	62						

PART 3   DIFFICULT COPY

	1'	2'	3'	5'	Page		1'	2'	3'	5'	Page
Telephone Innovations	x		x		75	Quartz			x	x	84
Methanol			x	x	76	Financial Statements	x		x		85
Acupuncture			x	x	76	Celebrating the New					
Trademarks	x		x		77	Year			x	x	86
Diction	x		x		77	Marconi	x		x		87
Petroleum			x	x	78	Selecting Meeting Sites			x	x	88
Graffiti			x	x	78	Model Railroads	x		x		89
Golf	x		x		79	Federal Reserve System			x	x	90
Apricots	x		x		79	Point-of-Sale Systems	x		x		91
Genealogy			x	x	80	Charcoal			x	x	92
Reducing Office Noise	x		x		81	Marketing Meetings	x		x		93
The Fireplace	x		x		81	Report to Shareholders			x	x	94
Soccer			x	x	82	Security for Loans	x		x		95
Japanese Flower						Temporary Employees			x	x	96
Arranging	x		x		83						

DRILLS

Keystroking Techniques

	Page		Page		Page
Specific Rows	5	Shift Key and Caps Lock Key	33	Adjacent Keys	63
Balance-Hand, One-Hand, and Double-Letter Words	11	Specific Keys	35	Letter, Word, or Combination Response	67
High-Frequency and Low-Frequency Words	17	Double-Letters, One-Hand Words, Common Phrases	41	Numbers and Symbols	71
Space Bar	19	Shift Key	47	Rough-Draft Copy	73
Left-Hand and Right-Hand Words	25	High-Frequency Words	53	Difficult Words	75
Tab Key	31	Shift Key and Caps Lock Key	59	Difficult Words	81
				Punctuation Marks	87
				Numbers and Symbols	91

Pyramid Paragraphs

Page	Page	Page
9	51	79
15	57	85
23	61	89
29	65	93
39	69	95
45		

Guided Writing Sentences

Page	Page	Page
7	27	49
13	37	77
21	43	83

PREFACE

Triple-Controlled Timed Writings, Third Edition, contains all new drills and new and revised timed writings. This book is intended to be a supplementary source of material used to improve straight copy performance and to measure progression at all levels of keyboarding.

This book is organized into three parts and contains three distinct categories of timed writings—EASY, AVERAGE, and DIFFICULT. The EASY timings are suitable for the beginner who has just mastered the keyboard as well as for the experienced keyboardist who wishes to regain or increase speed. The AVERAGE writings can be used to build the performance of the beginner gradually to that of the expert. The DIFFICULT writings may be used by the more advanced keyboardist to improve performance or by the average keyboardist to improve speed and accuracy levels. One-minute, three-minute, and five-minute timings are included in all three parts of this book. The EASY part of this book also contains two-minute timings.

Within each category, the timings are triple-controlled for their syllable intensity, average word length, and percentage of high frequency words. Research shows that fewer than 1300 words make up approximately 80 percent of our written language.* The frequency of use of these words provides the parameters of the word frequency control. The triple-control parameters for EASY, AVERAGE, and DIFFICULT timings are shown in the chart below.

	Easy	Average	Difficult
Syllable Intensity	1.2	1.5	1.8
Average Word Length (Strokes)	5.1	5.7	6.3
Percent of High Frequency Words	90.0	80.0	70.0

Although research has shown that straight copy is preferred for building speed, reality cannot be ignored. Therefore, proper nouns are found occasionally in some timings, and writings containing rough-draft, script, and statistical copy are included in the AVERAGE and DIFFICULT sections of this book. In addition, all timings contain every letter of the alphabet.

Drills and preliminary material are provided throughout the book with various types of reaches such as adjacent keys, difficult reaches, balanced hand, opposite hand, and low-frequency words included. Brief directions are given for each drill and skill-building exercise. Short reminders regarding proper posture, proper movement of arms and wrists, and the elimination of excess motion are also given in the drill work.

Guided writing sentences and pyramid paragraphs are included for speed building. Students are encouraged to "drop back" to easier material often as they proceed through the book since this has been shown to be a positive skill builder. A text-file diskette (TA05CH751, TA05CH811, TA05CH881), which contains selected timed writings from this book, is available for use with South-Western's MicroPace–Universal Timed Writing Program. The MicroPace program paces keystroking systematically and measures keystroking speed and accuracy.

The timings in this book cover a variety of subjects to enhance concentration while keyboarding. Instructors are encouraged to use the timings as a stimulus to keyboard composition by asking students to react to the timings. We also hope that students gain some interesting insights from the subject matter of the timings.

---

*The basic research on which *Triple Controlled Timed Writings* is based is a study by Lessenberry and Robinson who used as a source the word studies of Dewey, Thorndike-Lorge, Horn-Peterson, and Silverthorn.

PART 1

EASY COPY

The drill material in Part 1 provides speed and technique drills with reinforcement on keystroking, response patterns, and machine parts.

Goals for each drill are included to improve keystroking power.

Part 1 includes 1', 2', 3', and 5' triple-controlled timed writings of easy difficulty (syllable intensity, 1.23; average word length, 5.1; high-frequency words, 90%).

KEYSTROKING DRILL

Key the entire drill; repeat if time permits.

Line: 70 characters

Goal: Use a steady stroke throughout the drill.

Home-Row Keys
a; sl dk fj a;sldkfj a;sldkfj a;sldkfj a;sldkfj a;sldkfj a;sldkfj ghgh
flags glass asks hall lass fall half dash glad ask jag sag dad lad has
glass a half had has dad lad a has lad gas dad half a glass ask lad as
dish hash ask lads sass wash glass had dad had gag hall glass hag dash

Third-Row Keys
uj u rf r tf t ik i er e jy j ed e ol o ws w pq pq tee quote trip were
to it you toy tip row ire yet prey quit were type riot tire tree quote
pop quit you to it quote wipe peer pop you your yet pipe quiet top tip
try type upper row were root quote wet your rot report ripe quote quit

First-Row Keys
mj m vf v nj n bf b ,k , cd c .l . xs x za z /; / zxcv bn m,./ bn nb.
azure sox six dab babe zinc man nix mix cave axe excite on bobby vixen
mix jinx axe cozy named men brave van nanny lamb zip cave calm man ban
box back azure gaze lazy mix nix sax vex cache boon noon moon cede axe

	gwam	1'	2'	3'
HOPE	All of those who have reached their goals and all of those who will	14	7	4
	do so in the future have at least one trait in common, and that is hope.	28	14	9
	Hope draws power from a great trust in basic good that is living in all	43	22	14
	of us. Hope will open a door where despair will close it. Hope will	57	28	19
	find what can be done rather than complain about what cannot be done.	71	35	24
	Hope will move one to keep trying when it would be so easy to quit.	85	42	28
	Hope will accept small gains knowing that even long journeys must still	99	50	33
	start with a first step. Those who do reach their goals, whether they	113	57	38
	be extremely large or very small, see a setback not as a failure, but as	128	64	43
	a chance fostered by hope to realize final goals.	138	69	46

gwam	1'	1	2	3	4	5	6	7	8	9	10	11	12	13	14
	2'		1		2		3		4		5		6		7

TEMPORARY EMPLOYEES

For centuries, the custom has been for people to work the identical number of hours daily and days weekly. This may remain the typical circumstance, but a relatively unique type of employee, the temporary worker, is becoming popular. Temporary employees are individuals who work half days, a few days weekly, or a few weeks a year. Temporary help agencies originated and developed this phenomenon into an important component in our labor force.

From the standpoint of the employee, a temporary worker may work as often as he or she desires. To refuse a particular assignment does not take on the importance of refusing a permanent position. Workers forced to work shorter hours in their regular jobs can take advantage of temporary work opportunities. For seasonal workers, temporary work offers an attractive alternative to unemployment. Temporary work also provides a challenge for those who like change.

For the employer, temporary employees offer a variety of quality skills but do not require the costly advertising and screening needed for permanent employees. A temporary agency assumes the payroll expenses, and fringe benefits are lower because the employee is hired only when he or she is needed. In general, temporary employees make up an efficient labor pool ready to serve nearby firms. The future of temporary employees appears to be good with rich advantages for employees and employers.

	gwam	3'	5'
	4	2	59
	7	4	61
	10	6	63
	14	9	65
	17	10	67
	21	12	69
	24	14	71
	27	16	73
	30	18	74
	33	20	76
	37	22	79
	40	24	81
	43	26	83
	47	28	85
	50	30	87
	53	32	89
	57	34	91
	60	36	93
	61	37	93
	64	38	95
	67	40	97
	70	42	99
	73	44	101
	76	46	102
	79	48	104
	82	50	106
	85	51	108
	88	53	110
	92	55	112
	94	57	113

MURPHY'S LAW

Murphy's Law states that if anything can go wrong, it will. Once you become aware of this law, it will seem as if it is working in your life on a daily basis. There are many examples of this law at work. If food is spilled at the table, chances are that it will land on your clothing, which will be, no doubt, of a different color. The clothes will not only be clean, but brand new as well. Further, your power will go off just when you must trust your clock radio to get you up in the morning for an appointment.

If you explain something so clearly that no one can misunderstand, someone will. When a bargain occurs, you have no money; an item always will go on sale after you just bought it last week. You will remember a birthday one day too late, and everything will take longer than you think it will. The car will not start when you are late for work, and the rain always seems to fall on your picnic. You can be sure that the very thing you plan to do first must be shifted to last. The effect of this law is when nothing can go wrong, it will.

	3'	5'
	4	3 45
	9	5 48
	14	8 50
	18	11 53
	23	14 56
	28	17 59
	33	19 62
	34	21 63
	39	23 65
	44	26 68
	48	29 71
	53	32 74
	58	35 77
	63	37 80
	67	40 82
	70	42 84

THE ART OF CONVERSATION

Would you like to learn to converse in a better manner? Here are some tips to help you. Conversation is more than just talk; it means to listen as well. Pay close attention to what the other person is say-ing rather than thinking about what you plan to say. You will become so engrossed in what is being said that you will not have time to be self-conscious. Do not be restless and allow your eyes to roam around the room, or it will be difficult for the other person to talk to you.

When it comes time for you to talk, learn to talk about those things that interest the other person; you will never have to fret about being ignored. Leave out facts which are not important; the secret to being a bore is to tell everything. Talk about one subject long enough for there to be give and take about it. Do not jump from one topic to another. Do not interrupt your topic to tell a story; people who tell jokes are not as popular as you may think. Use logic, be clear, and be to the point.

	3'	5'
	4	3 42
	9	5 45
	14	8 48
	18	11 51
	23	14 54
	28	17 56
	32	20 59
	37	22 62
	42	25 65
	47	28 68
	52	31 71
	56	34 73
	61	37 76
	66	39 79
	66	39 79

gwam 3' | 1 | 2 | 3 | 4 | 5 |
5' | 1 | 2 | 3 |

PYRAMID PARAGRAPHS

Line: 70 characters
Goal: Build speed. Key each line of the first paragraph within 15", 12", or 10"; break through your speed ceiling. Then repeat the goal for the second paragraph.

Key: 1' timings on the paragraphs. If you finish a line before the time interval is called, continue to the next line; if not, repeat the unfinished line.

	gwam 1'
When you are new on the job, it is natural to feel	10
strange and uncomfortable. You will not know the job.	21
The way you handle yourself the first several days can set	33
the tone for your relationship with other workers. It is best	45
to listen and learn all you can about your job. You should try to	58
be a part of the work team. You can be a trusted member of the team.	72
Many office workers today are involved directly in	10
information processing work. This work can cover data	21
entry, operations, or programming. In these different job	33
areas, technical training is required. All workers should try	45
to understand the reasons for using information processing and the	58
services provided by the information processing center to departments.	72

gwam 1' | 1 | 2 | 3 | 4 | 5 | 6 | 7 | 8 | 9 | 10 | 11 | 12 | 13 | 14 |

SECURITY FOR LOANS

	gwam 1'		3'
Security for loans involves different forms.	8	3	65
Often cash loans are obtained that are either	18	6	68
secured or unsecured. Whenever a secured loan	27	9	71
is considered, the borrower pledges some personal	37	12	74
property to the lender to guarantee repayment of	47	16	78
the loan. Property normally used as security for	57	19	81
loans is referred to as collateral. Bonds, stocks,	68	23	84
automobiles, houses, jewelry, and insurance	76	25	87
policies are some examples of collateral. The	86	29	90
purpose of the collateral is to protect the lender	96	32	94
if the borrower fails to repay the loan. The	105	35	97
lender has the privilege of selling the collateral	115	38	100
if the promissory note has not been repaid by	125	41	103
the maturity date. Another form of security	134	44	106
is the loan endorsement that requires the borrower	144	48	110
to obtain another individual, called a cosigner,	154	51	113
to assume responsibility for the loan if the	163	54	116
borrower fails to repay it. Both borrower and	172	57	119
cosigner sign the promissory note and both are	181	60	122
obligated by the note.	186	62	124

GUIDED WRITING SENTENCES

Line: 60 characters
Goal: Build speed. Key each sentence in 12" or 10".

Key: 30" or 1' timings on the sentences. If you finish a sentence before the time interval is called, go to the next sentence. For each new timing, continue from last complete sentence keyed.

		gwam per line	12"	10"
1	Their software is ready.		24	29
2	Does the boy like to play?		26	31
3	Did he use a quicker stroke?		28	34
4	Be alert to the computer plan.		30	36
5	Put the box on the desk, please.		32	38
6	That program needs to be improved.		34	41
7	Please lend a hand to those in need.		36	43
8	Add one phone to your home and my car.		38	46
9	When did the five boys go to their work?		40	48
10	They must fix in mind all goals they seek.		42	50
11	Ship today beans and peas at the best price.		44	53
12	The person who wants to win a prize must work.		46	55

gwam	1'	1	2	3	4	5	6	7	8	9
	30"	2	4	6	8	10	12	14	16	18

	gwam	1'	2'	3'

THIRD FINGER, LEFT HAND

Why is an engagement and a wedding ring put on the third finger of the left hand? This has not always been the case; even the thumb was once a choice. A major reason to use the left hand is that this hand is not as active as the right hand. The third finger is also the least used out of the ten. In prior times, some actually thought that the third finger had very sensitive nerves that went directly to the heart. Whatever the case, one must realize that the third finger will take quite an active part in expressing love in our day and will likely do so in future times to come.

gwam 1'	2'	3'
13	7	4
27	14	9
42	21	14
56	28	19
70	35	23
84	42	28
98	49	33
112	56	37
117	59	39

	gwam	1'	2'	3'

BOXING DAY

Boxing Day does not refer to a fight between two boxers. This day is a type of holiday in England and some of the nations in the Commonwealth. It will take place on the first working day after Christmas. A box with a gift in it will be given to a delivery boy, the postman, a maid, or some worker close to the family or firm. Not that it is just a day of giving, for it is a sort of legal respite from work in these member nations. The day could be a quiet one as trains may not run, cafes and stores can be closed down, organizations may not meet, and public services are reduced or cut. If you are going to be in one of the nations of the Commonwealth just after Christmas, keep this day in mind when you make your plans.

gwam 1'	2'	3'
13	7	4
27	14	9
41	21	14
56	28	19
70	35	23
85	42	28
99	50	33
113	57	38
127	64	42
141	71	47
146	73	49

gwam	1'	1	2	3	4	5	6	7	8	9	10	11	12	13	14
	2'		1		2		3		4		5		6		7	

**REPORT TO
SHARE-
HOLDERS**

Following a year of challenge and opportunity, Metropolitan Bank's | 4 | 3 | 79
Board of Directors is happy to report an earnings increase of 9.2%. As- | 9 | 6 | 82
sets totaled $31,792,061; liabilities, $28,017,734; and owners' equity, | 14 | 8 | 85
$3,774,327. Net income of $351,714 represents a 1.16% return on assets. | 19 | 11 | 88
As a result of this performance, the Board of Directors has again de- | 24 | 14 | 90
clared a $.10 per share cash dividend and a 10% stock dividend, payable | 28 | 17 | 93
February 28 to 746 shareholders of record on February 11. The cash | 33 | 20 | 96
dividend will be paid on total shares outstanding after the stock divi- | 38 | 23 | 99
dend has been issued. | 39 | 23 | 100

Maintaining a profit margin regardless of unprecedented high in- | 43 | 26 | 102
terest expense required careful scrutiny of this expense and a balanced | 48 | 29 | 105
loan portfolio. Even though the prime rate reached 20% in February and | 53 | 32 | 108
21.5% in December, after an interim decline, the state's usury statutes | 58 | 35 | 111
restricted rates on many loans to 12%. Because of a federal override, | 62 | 37 | 114
14% was charged later in the year. Interest costs on certificates of | 67 | 40 | 116
deposit exceeded the legal maximum rate, and net interest margin in- | 72 | 43 | 119
creased to 8.75%, or $489,076, by the year-end. This result was obtained | 77 | 46 | 122
by a liquidity strategy that curbed interest expense. | 80 | 48 | 124

Facing declining interest rates, the Directors adopted a nonaggres- | 85 | 51 | 127
sive strategy in bidding for large certificates of deposit; this reduced | 89 | 54 | 130
the interest expense and improved the net interest margin. It also con- | 94 | 57 | 133
tributed to a 4.4% decline in total deposits. The most relevant factor | 99 | 59 | 136
in improving the net interest margin and the earnings record was the | 104 | 62 | 138
bank's favorable ratio of demand deposits, which represented $13,448,617 | 108 | 65 | 141
or 48.6% of the total deposits. The advent on January 1 of checking | 113 | 68 | 144
accounts that earn interest will alter the deposit mix and will mean | 118 | 71 | 147
that service charges and interest on loans will have to be maintained | 122 | 73 | 150
at a level that will cover the expenses of these accounts. | 127 | 76 | 152

gwam 3' | 1 | 2 | 3 | 4 | 5
     5' | 1 | 2 | 3

CORPORATE OWNERSHIP

	gwam	3'	5'

A corporation is a form of business that is owned by a group of people. The state gives it power to act as if it were a single person by means of a charter. In a sense, a corporation is a make-believe person which has been made possible by state law. Ownership is divided into parts called shares. When people buy a share of stock, they are part owners of the firm and are known as shareholders. They elect the board members, who develop the plans to guide the firm and then appoint officers to carry out the plans. The officers are the managers of the firm.

The two main types of stock are common and preferred. People who own common stock share in the profits by means of dividends. The dividend rate may vary from year to year. They also share in the management of the firm by the right to vote. Dividends usually must be paid on preferred stock before they are paid on common stock. A dividend is often a set rate based on the face value of the stock. In most cases, people who own preferred stock do not have the right to vote.

gwam column values: 4/3/45, 9/6/48, 14/8/50, 19/11/53, 23/14/56, 28/17/59, 33/20/62, 38/23/65, 42/25/67, 47/28/70, 52/31/73, 56/34/76, 61/37/79, 65/39/81, 70/42/84

THE MOST SERENE REPUBLIC OF SAN MARINO

	gwam	3'	5'

The country of San Marino is well known as the oldest republic in the world. It had its start in the fourth century, and it is found in a place near the Adriatic Sea. It has but a single country to its border, which is Italy. It is less than twenty-four square miles in size and has as few as thirty-thousand people. This nation has known some political problems through the years; but the country has a fine record as being a nation that has been able to live in peace, since it has kept out of a major war for many years.

The nation has a very high number of people who are able to read or write. Some of the products of this country are grains and fruits. Lime, wheat, stone, and hides are among the exports. However, the export for which this small nation is best known and which provides a large amount of funds is the postage stamp. A person who is born in this land is always considered to be one of its citizens, and such a person has the right to vote no matter where that person will live or how long he or she may stay out of the country.

gwam column values: 4/3/45, 9/6/48, 14/8/51, 19/11/54, 23/14/57, 28/17/60, 33/20/62, 36/21/64, 40/24/67, 45/27/70, 49/30/72, 54/32/75, 59/35/78, 63/38/81, 68/41/83, 71/43/85

gwam 3' 1 2 3 4 5
     5' 1 2 3

PYRAMID PARAGRAPHS

Line: 70 characters
Goal: Build speed. Key each line of the first paragraph within 15", 12", or 10"; break through your speed ceiling. Then repeat the goal for the second paragraph.

Key: 1' timings on the paragraphs. If you finish a line before the time interval is called, continue to the next line; if not, repeat the unfinished line.

	gwam 1'
The high school senior has a difficult decision to	10
make in selecting a college to attend. This choice is	21
the first of four major decisions seniors will make in the	33
next five years. The other three decisions are major, career,	45
and mate. Although the stakes might be high, seniors shouldn't be	58
afraid of the process. Choosing a college should be a growth process.	72
Computers today are becoming so widely used in all	10
phases of the workplace and the home. They help solve	21
problems. To understand how a computer can do this, first	33
you need to understand the process of solving problems. Learn	45
the specific steps that will lead to a desired solution or result.	58
Solving problems with computers today is very common in everyday life.	72

gwam 1' | 1 | 2 | 3 | 4 | 5 | 6 | 7 | 8 | 9 | 10 | 11 | 12 | 13 | 14 |

MARKETING MEETINGS

	gwam 1'	3'
The meetings market mushroomed during the last decade. Meetings	13	4 | 97
grew in size, duration, and number as the ubiquitous baby boomer swelled	28	9 |101
the ranks of corporations and associations. The market is full of	41	14 |106
well-educated meeting executives. Over 57% and 15% of all planners are	55	18 |111
part-timers working for corporations and associations, respectively.	69	23 |115
Approximately 65 out of 100 association planners and 52 out of 100	83	28 |120
corporate planners are women. Most are between 35 and 55 years of age,	97	32 |125
and 54% of the corporate and 41% of the association planners earn over	111	37 |129
$35,000 annually. Some 68% of the corporate and 72% of the association	126	42 |134
planners have at least four years of experience in the field.	**138**	46 |138
It is said that the Fortune 1000 companies will spend over $41	13	50 |142
billion on meetings this year. Last year attendees, exhibitors, and	26	55 |147
sponsors spent over $44.5 billion. An average firm spent over $605,000,	41	60 |152
including attendee expenses. A typical association spent $543,000,	55	64 |156
excluding delegate expenses. One year ago, over 22.5 million business	69	69 |161
travelers made at least 74 million business trips to participate in	82	73 |166
meetings. If we assume that all individuals earn $35,000 as a yearly	96	78 |170
salary and spent two days away from their jobs, then another $29 billion	111	83 |175
was spent in manpower sending people to meetings. In the near future,	125	88 |180
meetings will be even more essential to corporations and associations.	**139**	92 |184

gwam 1' | 1 | 2 | 3 | 4 | 5 | 6 | 7 | 8 | 9 | 10 | 11 | 12 | 13 | 14 |
3' | 1 | 2 | 3 | 4 | 5 |

PYRAMID PARAGRAPHS

Line: 70 characters
Goal: Build speed. Key each line of the paragraph within 15", 12", or 10".

Return with minimum motion; keep eyes on copy.
Key: 1' timing on the paragraph. If you finish a line before the time interval is called, continue to the next line; if not, repeat the unfinished line.

	gwam 1'
Keep your talk very short.	5
If one says he or she will make	11
the long tale short, he or she has	18
just as good as said that now the tale	26
will be very long. It is hard to be brief	34
when we tell the tale, yet we know that is the	43
best way to speak. Can you learn to be brief when	53
you speak? Yes, you can. However, this will call for	64
many thoughts as you now plan what you wish to say. Think	76
before you speak. Try to make your next talk brief and clear.	88

gwam 1' | 1 | 2 | 3 | 4 | 5 | 6 | 7 | 8 | 9 | 10 | 11 | 12 | 13 |

---

		gwam	1'	2'	3'
PERKS	Perk is a short word for perquisite, which is a benefit given to		13	6	4
	top management. In short, perks are the extras that are made available		27	14	9
	to top employees in a firm. Their real purpose is to make all of the		41	21	14
	strains and stresses of a busy work life worthwhile. Other times they		57	28	19
	are used to attract a top worker to a job or to keep one with a firm.		70	35	23
	Some of the common perks are a free car, membership in a club, a discount		85	42	28
	on merchandise, use of a company plane, and, of course, free counseling		99	50	33
	to keep it all in order. These items may be subject to state and federal		114	57	38
	tax, and the government tries to see that they are reported as income.		128	64	43

		gwam	1'	2'	3'
PLUTO	The planet Pluto is quite small. Our earth is approximately five		13	7	4
	times larger in size. Despite its small size, Pluto is very inter-		27	13	9
	esting to the study of science. It is on the outside of our solar sys-		41	20	14
	tem, and it has the least usual orbit in our system. Not much is known		55	28	18
	about this body, but it is thought to be cold, dark, and dead. Its moon		70	35	23
	is about one-third the size of the planet. As the moon does a turn,		84	42	28
	this turn is in the same pattern as Pluto's turn; thus, the same points		98	49	33
	of the two will always face each other. Found in the third decade of		112	56	37
	this century, it can be seen only with a very large telescope and when		126	63	42
	the ability to view is at its best. Just like the earth, it may have		140	70	47
	ice at the top and bottom of its body which may become large or small		154	77	51
	with the changes of each season.		161	80	53

gwam 1' | 1 | 2 | 3 | 4 | 5 | 6 | 7 | 8 | 9 | 10 | 11 | 12 | 13 | 14 |
2' | 1 | 2 | 3 | 4 | 5 | 6 | 7 |

Charcoal is a fuel often selected by ^*outdoor* cooks, espe~*c*ially   4 | 3 | 69

at picnics and bar~*b*cues. Its clean flame and outstanding   8 | 5 | 72

ability to r~*a*diate heat /# make it particularly effective. Con-   12 | 7 | 74

t~*r*olling the temperature~*s* of the fire is easy with the small ^   16 | 10 | 77

uniformly size~*d* briquettes. Charcoal is relatively low in   20 | 12 | 79

~*cost* ~~price~~ and can usually be found in a grocery store or drugstore.   24 | 15 | 82

^*An additional* ~~Another~~ advantage of charcoal is that it burns with little   29 | 17 | 84

residue.   29 | 18 | 84

~~Historically,~~ *stet* charcoal was produced in numerous areas   33 | 20 | 87

by making cupola-shaped woodpiles approximately twenty feet   34 | 22 | 89

high and thirty feet across. Each woodpile was /# covered with   41 | 25 | 91

straw and earth ^ and a fire was started in the hollow center   45 | 27 | 94

of the cupola. After the woodpile had been burned to the   49 | 29 | 96

point that most t~*a*rry and ^*volatile* materials had dissipated, workers   53 | 32 | 99

wearing protective footwear ^*quickly* ascended the cupola to carry off   58 | 35 | 102

the smol~*d*ering material, now become charcoal. Proper timing   62 | 37 | 104

at this stage was very important bec~*au*se it affected the   66 | 40 | 106

quality ~*of the product.*   67 | 41 | 107

Charcoal can be obtained from many inexpensive /# materials ^   71 | 43 | 110

including corn cobs, rice hulls, and various ^*vegetable* products. How-   76 | 45 | 112

ever, wood is usually the principal material. The processed   80 | 48 | 115

charcoal is approximat~*e*ly one-fourth the size of the original   84 | 50 | 117

piece of wood, but its resistance to decay is much greater.   88 | 53 | 119

Charcoal also pos~*s*esses the ability to absorb gases, and thus   92 | 55 | 122

it is used extensive ly in filtering poisonous gases during   96 | 57 | 124

wartime. The development of charcoal is an exampl~*e* of the   100 | 60 | 127

^*early* exploitation of fire and heat to convert a raw material into   105 | 62 | 129

a more valuable product. ^*Once this is done,* The product can be utilized as a   110 | 66 | 132

raw material for other processes.   112 | 67 | 134

TREE RINGS

Many of us have been quite amazed to learn that we could find the age of a tree by making a note of the number of rings in the trunk. Most trees in this part of the world add new growth in much the same way each year which gives us the chance to learn their ages and even more about their inside growth. This process will start when new tissue is added just inside the bark by a very small line of cells called the cambium. With the coming of spring, each of these cells will start its division. Those on the outside go to the phloem of the plant. This phloem is a narrow line of bark. From the inside come straw-like cells that carry the needed water from the ground. These are called xylem. A sharp line is found between the converging cells. This line forms the annual ring that will tell us that yet another year has gone by. The cause of this annual event of growth results from a wide range of forces of nature, and within the annual lines are found much important and interesting information for the average person as well as science.

gwam	3'	5'
	4	3 45
	9	5 47
	14	8 50
	18	11 53
	23	14 56
	28	17 59
	33	20 62
	37	22 64
	42	25 67
	47	28 70
	52	31 73
	56	34 76
	61	37 79
	66	39 81
	70	42 84

THE POTATO

The potato is one of the eight main food crops of the world. It is different from the others in that the part that can be eaten is found below the ground. Cultivation of the plant is dated to the second century. At one time, it was thought that it was an aphrodisiac. To this day, some people carry a piece of it with them to guard against rheumatism. Ireland was once well known for this food, but it was the potato famine that brought many of these people to our land many years ago.

In recent years, some people have decided not to eat potatoes very often because they think that potatoes have too many calories; but this is not true. The potato is equal in this respect to an apple of the same size. What is more, they are full of top quality food value. They may be prepared in a number of ways; for example, they may be baked, boiled, or stuffed. As a result, it is common to see them on many a table each day. They come in many a shape and size, but the two types usually found in most stores across this country are the round, white ones and the oblong russets. They are of good quality all year long.

gwam	3'	5'
	4	3 47
	9	5 50
	14	8 53
	19	11 56
	23	14 59
	28	16 62
	33	20 65
	37	22 67
	42	25 70
	47	28 73
	51	31 76
	56	34 78
	61	36 81
	65	39 84
	70	42 87
	75	45 90

gwam 3' | 1 | 2 | 3 | 4 | 5 |
5' | 1 | 2 | 3 |

KEYSTROKING DRILL

Key each line twice; repeat if time permits.
Line: 70 characters

Goal: Keep hands quiet, fingers curved and upright. Concentrate on location of the numbers and symbols as you key.

Numbers and Symbols

The Federal Deposit Insurance Corporation (FDIC) limit is $100,000.00.
The cost of gasoline rose from $.879 on July 26 to $1.49 on August 13.
In a 564-page report, this year's profit was to be over $13.9 million.
Fraud task forces in 32 cities hired 104 attorneys and 174 FBI agents.

The company will give more than 3,825 hourly employees $1,976 bonuses.
The recent $7 per barrel increase to $28 would cost about 39,654 jobs.
A loss of $58 million was due to the closing of 37 stores on March 24.
A note for $301,475 dated 9/6/89 at 12% interest was found in the box.

Her first novel, Your Business Attitude, had sales of 165,382 in 1991.
If you add 25 + 60 + 5 - 10 + 30 - 40 + 20 - 5 - 15, your total is 70.
Invoice #973520 requested seven 60-gallon drums and 48 #3 cans of oil.
The S&L funds valued at $1,409,372,658 gained $571,320.69 in interest.

POINT-OF-SALE SYSTEMS

	gwam	1'	3'

Individuals employed often
~~People~~ who are ~~working~~ in stores ~~frequently~~ use computers in [12 | 4 | 79]
special
point-of-sale systems. These^systems are computerized systems for [27 | 9 | 84]
clients their
recording sales as ~~customers~~ pay for ~~his or her~~ merchandise. One [19 | 13 | 87]
includes
example of ~~department~~ stores that uses point^of^sale systems ~~are~~ [50 | 17 | 91]
their
department stores^department^stores are known for ~~its~~ point^of^sale [65 | 21 | 96]
registers are ed
~~systems~~. Registers are classified/not as computers but ~~as~~ connections [79 | 26 | 101]
a store's a
to ~~the main~~ computer. Whenever a customer purchases merchandise, an [93 | 31 | 106]
device wand
unique ~~tool~~ called a ~~scanner~~ scans over a special tag attached to the [107 | 36 | 110]
Every
merchandise. ~~The~~ tag identifies a code specifying the item ~~to be~~ [119 | 40 | 114]
a store's
purchased. The code is electronically forwarded to ~~the~~ computer which [135 | 45 | 119]
and records the transaction
determines the price of the item. ~~The~~ computer then transmits the [153 | 51 | 126]
calculate
price to the register to ~~compute~~ the amount owed by the customer. The [168 | 56 | 131]
computer automatically utilizes the transaction information to adjust [182 | 61 | 135]
its regarding the quantity stet
~~the~~ inventory records of the item in stock. as all ~~store~~ registers [201 | 67 | 141]
t
are connected to the same computer it usually does not mater which [214 | 71 | 146]
register a customer uses to pay for ~~the~~ merchandise. [224 | 75 | 149]

KEYSTROKING DRILL

Key the entire drill once; repeat if time permits.   *Line:* 70 characters   *Goal:* Operate on the stroke level; maintain steady rhythm.

Balanced-Hand Words

me he am go so do an us if by or it is to of may for and the go for it but pay sir due me own did box when an than make them the with rob rid work such forms then wish paid name held both they also mane city that and the may go to due men it them six work box fox odd right field bye

One-Hand Words

we set few tax in be on no as at up are my set get him far lop pup dad dear were best only date card area kiln case ever rate fact hum kin as fast tax ever wart only lip state get in as joy rates sad fade ion pop cast loop upon area after pop cases few pip crab taste grass at him on

Double-Letter Words

week soon feel call well full need good been will too took see fee boo less books fill bill shall three offer issue root feet seed wood steel food feed reed good hood leer peep peer smell ball beer weep shall nee offer lass less jeep purr off muff offer keen loon thee boon boom soot

	gwam	1'	2'	3'
ABOUT TO MISS A DEADLINE?	Even though you could be a well-organized person whose work is often	14	7	5
	done on time and is under control, it sometimes happens that you sud-	28	14	9
	denly realize that you are going to miss a major deadline. You feel	41	21	14
	full of guilt and anxiety. You feel as if you are going to let other	55	28	18
	persons down, which is very hard to accept. Given these feelings, the	70	35	23
	first step is to warn the people involved, even if this is a difficult	84	42	28
	thing to do. You owe it to others to let them know in time to adjust	98	49	33
	their plans. Second, give the project all your effort. You may be	111	56	37
	late, but then who knows, you may finish just in time.	122	61	41

	gwam	1'	2'	3'
CINDER CONES	Vulcan is a small island near Sicily. This island was thought to	13	7	4
	be the home of Vulcan, a blacksmith, and is the home and name source of	28	14	9
	volcanoes. One of the main and most simple volcanoes is the cinder cone.	43	21	14
	It is usually small in size and forms from lava that comes from just	56	28	19
	one small area in the ground. After the hot matter has moved quickly	70	35	23
	into the air, it forms small, firm pieces that extend and fall as cin-	84	42	28
	ders around the open space to form a cone. All of these will have a	98	49	33
	similar shape at the top and are often less than a thousand feet above	112	56	37
	the ground. These cones are located in many parts of the world.	125	63	42

gwam	1'	1	2	3	4	5	6	7	8	9	10	11	12	13	14
	2'	1		2		3		4		5		6		7	

**FEDERAL
RESERVE
SYSTEM**

Who is in charge of the management of our country's money supply? 4 | 3 | 74

The federal reserve system has this awesome responsibility. This system 9 | 5 | 77

has numerous supervisory, regulatory, and administrative functions. It 14 | 8 | 80

helps to direct the flow of credit to the nation's entire banking system, 19 | 11 | 83

fosters an orderly growth of our country's economy, and insures a stable 24 | 14 | 86

dollar. The federal reserve system meets these objectives mainly by 28 | 17 | 88

buying and selling government securities, lending money, and varying 33 | 20 | 91

the reserve allocations of member banks. The nation is divided into 37 | 22 | 94

districts, and a central bank is designated in each one. Over one half 42 | 25 | 97

of the banks in this nation belong to the federal reserve system. 46 | 28 | 99

The relationship of a federal reserve bank to its member banks is 51 | 30 | 102

very similar to a bank's relationship to its customers. Deposits are 55 | 33 | 104

accepted only from the member banks, and loans are made only to these 60 | 36 | 107

banks. A federal reserve bank can also perform the valuable function of 65 | 39 | 110

clearing checks between member banks in different cities. Procedures 69 | 41 | 113

have been devised to enable the fast return of out-of-town checks 74 | 44 | 116

to the banks on which they were drawn. Member banks maintain reserves 78 | 47 | 118

on deposit without interest, and they comply with federal statutes and 83 | 50 | 121

regulations relating to such matters as maintaining enough capital, re- 88 | 53 | 124

stricting investments, creating new branches, and reviewing the possi- 92 | 55 | 127

bility of mergers. 93 | 56 | 127

The system is managed by a seven-member Board of Governors. The 97 | 58 | 130

Board's membership is appointed by the President of the United States 102 | 61 | 132

and confirmed by the Senate. The Board manages the budget and the 106 | 64 | 135

responsibilities of the individual reserve banks, approves the appoint- 111 | 67 | 138

ment of every president of the reserve banks, and appoints several direc- 116 | 69 | 141

tors to each of the participating reserve banks. 119 | 71 | 143

gwam 3' | 1 | 2 | 3 | 4 | 5
5' | 1 | 2 | 3

CONSULATES

Consuls are found at embassies and consulates in most foreign nations. These men and women are asked by our government to live in a city in a foreign land and serve visiting citizens and business interests of our country. They can tell you of bad problems in places that you plan to see and can help you if a crisis should come about. If you are planning more than a short stay, or if you are in a place where civil unrest exists, it is wise to contact an office that is near so that you can stay in touch with a home source.

	3'	5'
	4	3 44
	9	5 47
	14	8 49
	19	11 52
	24	14 55
	28	17 58
	33	20 61
	35	21 62

If you are in legal straits, such as having a passport taken or lost, you should get in touch with a consul just as quickly as you can. A new passport can be issued to you in a short time. For a more serious matter, they will not act as lawyers, since this is not permitted. They cannot get you out of jail, but they will let you know of your rights. Should you lose any of your personal items, they can help you obtain additional funds and help you locate your family or your bank if needed.

	3'	5'
	39	24 64
	44	27 68
	49	30 71
	54	32 73
	59	35 76
	64	38 79
	68	41 82

COFFEE

The coffee tree is still found in a natural state in Africa, the place where it all started. Yemen was the first country to better the product so that it could be sold at a profit. Its effect was first seen by shepherds who found that goats in their charge did not rest well when they ate the plant. It was named for caffeine, which it has in considerable quantity. One story on how it came west says that after the Turks lost a war, they left the beans on the field; these were later found and were taken to the West.

	3'	5'
	4	3 43
	9	5 46
	14	8 49
	18	11 51
	23	14 54
	28	17 57
	33	20 60
	35	21 61

The first coffee house was seen in the city of London in the middle of the seventeenth century. It was not long before more than three thousand of these could be found in that city. They would create so many problems that the head of state realized the need to cut their activities. At one time, coffee was sold as a medical answer to all types of ills. In this country, the money spent on coffee has gone up to more than six billion dollars which is spent each year just for this drink.

	3'	5'
	39	24 64
	44	26 67
	48	29 70
	53	32 72
	58	35 75
	62	37 78
	67	40 81
	68	41 81

gwam 3' | 1 | 2 | 3 | 4 | 5 |
5' | 1 | 2 | 3 |

PYRAMID PARAGRAPHS

Line: 60 characters
Goal: Build speed. Key each line of the paragraph within 15", 12", or 10"; break through your speed ceiling.
Key: 1' timing on the paragraph. If you finish a line before the time interval is called, continue to the next line; if not, repeat the unfinished line.

	gwam	1'
While you are still in school,		6
your basic needs are provided by		13
an adult. In only a few years you		21
will be providing for your own basic		29
needs. You will search for a place to		38
live. You will need to furnish your new		48
home. Also you may want a new car. There		59
will be many other things you will need. At		71
this time you will be concerned about your own		83
needs and wants; these needs may change in time.		96

gwam 1' | 1 | 2 | 3 | 4 | 5 | 6 | 7 | 8 | 9 | 10 |

MODEL RAILROADS

	gwam 1'	3'	
For over a century and a half trains have fascinated people of all	13	4	98
age groups residing in many areas of the world. It is therefore not too	28	9	103
surprising that this affection spills over to include replicas of these	42	14	108
famous prototypes. Model railroad enthusiasts divide into three basic	57	19	112
groups. There are artisans who construct miniature representations and	71	24	117
layouts, and there are collectors who buy quality models. Naturally,	85	28	122
the largest group is composed of those who are content merely to admire	99	33	127
the beautiful replicas. There are also specific categories of interest.	114	38	132
Some train hobbyists are interested only in locomotives, while the ex-	128	43	136
pertise of many others lies in elaborate track layouts.	139	46	140
Because model railroading is a hobby that is enjoyed by many people	14	51	144
in almost every part of the world, a number of support systems are now	28	56	149
available to those who adopt this pastime. For example, many organiza-	42	60	154
tions supply realistic methods to propel model railways, including steam,	57	65	159
clockwork, friction, and electricity. In addition, groups and societies	71	70	164
commonly offer exhibits and clinics for train hobbyists. Some of these	86	75	168
groups also publish magazines that impart historical data and layout de-	100	80	173
signs, as well as other information of interest to those who build or	114	84	178
collect models. Finally, the love they share for these miniature rep-	128	89	183
licas very often forms bonds of friendship among model train buffs.	142	94	188

gwam 1' | 1 | 2 | 3 | 4 | 5 | 6 | 7 | 8 | 9 | 10 | 11 | 12 | 13 | 14 |
3' | 1 | 2 | 3 | 4 | 5 |

GUIDED WRITING SENTENCES

Line: 60 characters
Goal: Build speed. Key each sentence in 12" or 10".

Key: 30" or 1' timings on the sentences. If you finish a sentence before the time interval is called, go to the next sentence. For each new timing, continue from last complete sentence keyed.

		gwam per line	12"	10"
1	Know your strong points.		24	29
2	Sit up in an erect manner.		26	31
3	Travel by air can be costly.		28	34
4	Work as if the job were vital.		30	36
5	To listen is hard work at times.		32	38
6	The friend can be the best mirror.		34	41
7	Direct deposit is a real time saver.		36	43
8	A good habit will pay off in due time.		38	46
9	Be sure that you walk more than you sit.		40	48
10	The slick road and fog caused the problem.		42	50
11	Two feet on the ground means a shorter fall.		44	53
12	Make the work easy by putting your mind to it.		46	55

gwam 1'	1	2	3	4	5	6	7	8	9
30"	2	4	6	8	10	12	14	16	18

---

		gwam 1'	2'	3'

ADOBE

Adobe is the term for bricks made from dried clay. This material has been used for building in some parts of the world for many years. Today it is still used in the southern and western parts of our country and in other areas of the world where it is dry most of the year. Adobe is a good material to use because it is strong, and it will keep out the heat and cold. At the same time, it will keep the inside of the building at an even temperature. In addition, the bricks are easy to make. The correct type of clay is added to straw or something similar to form the bricks which are then left to dry.

gwam 1'	2'	3'
13	7	4
27	14	9
42	21	14
56	28	19
70	35	23
84	42	28
98	49	33
112	56	37
121	61	40

MAIL ORDER

Mail order has been a method of buying and selling goods for many years. It was a common means for many when travel was hard and communications were not good. In our time, there is a new shortcut to help the busy buyer place orders. First, one can phone toll free any time of the day or night. With a catalog in hand, the one who needs to buy must only give a stock number, a color, and a size. The consumer then gives a credit card number and an address to the person at the store. All one does is wait for the purchase to come. For some, this is luxury in shopping. For others, though, there is no equal to the joy of shopping in many stores before making that final choice.

gwam 1'	2'	3'
13	7	4
28	14	9
42	21	14
57	28	19
72	36	24
85	43	28
100	50	33
113	57	38
128	64	42
137	68	46

gwam 1'	1	2	3	4	5	6	7	8	9	10	11	12	13	14
2'		1		2		3		4		5		6		7	

SELECTING MEETING SITES

All work and no play can make Jack and Jane very dull. This adage · 4 | 3 | 82

holds true for meeting attendees, and many convention planners recognize · 9 | 6 | 85

it. The fundamental leisure activities primary to the success of a · 14 | 8 | 87

meeting usually include golf, free time, tennis, and tours. Corpora- · 18 | 11 | 90

tions are attracted to golf, free time, and tennis; association attendees · 23 | 14 | 93

identify with free time, golf, and tours. Free time and tours are most · 28 | 17 | 96

likely preferred since various individuals use association meetings as an · 33 | 20 | 99

opportunity to plan a vacation with the family. Paradoxically, while · 37 | 22 | 101

these activities are extremely important to making a meeting successful, · 42 | 25 | 104

they are also usually low priorities when the planners are looking for a · 47 | 28 | 107

site. · 48 | 28 | 107

Convenience to travelers and overall costs are consistently of · 52 | 31 | 110

utmost importance to planners. The chief reasons for choosing a hotel · 58 | 35 | 113

includes proximity to the meeting, efficiency of registration, quality · 61 | 37 | 116

of food and location of restaurants, and proximity to the airport. The · 66 | 40 | 119

key factors for selecting a site are related to the hotels, including · 71 | 42 | 121

food and beverage, followed by air travel. There are apparently few · 75 | 45 | 124

differences in the priorities of corporate and association planners. The · 80 | 48 | 127

availability of hotel rooms and distance of the hotel from the meeting · 85 | 51 | 130

site are the top two criteria for selecting a hotel. Hotel room rates · 90 | 54 | 132

and the cost of meeting space are secondary. · 93 | 56 | 135

Often an association planner selects the site first, then he or she · 97 | 58 | 137

locates the hotel. Many do not select destinations in their states or · 102 | 61 | 140

in nearby cities. Although most meetings are seldom overseas or on · 106 | 64 | 143

cruise ships, this will probably·change in the immediate future. In · 111 | 67 | 146

regards to property classification, meetings are held generally in mid- · 116 | 69 | 148

town hotels and at resorts. A typical meeting can occur during any · 120 | 72 | 151

season, and most planners often schedule it between Sunday and Thursday. · 125 | 75 | 154

Convention bureaus use every opportunity to influence the selec- · 130 | 78 | 157

tion process by planners. · 132 | 79 | 158

gwam 3' | 1 | 2 | 3 | 4 | 5 |
5' | 1 | 2 | 3 |

THE CONSTITUTION

	gwam 3'	5'
More than two hundred years ago, the leaders of this nation met to	4	3 47
discuss and agree upon a form of law by which all citizens would live.	9	6 50
The new nation had been through a long, hard war to win its freedom, and	14	8 53
people still had a distrust of big government. Men from each of the	19	11 56
states, each quite anxious to protect his own area, talked and wrote	23	14 59
his lines in the hot, humid weather. The weeks led to months as the	28	17 61
men would not agree over what the new document would say and what it	33	20 64
would not say. Then, at long last, an agreement was reached. Few men	37	22 67
were really happy with the results because there had been much give and	42	25 70
take by each man.	43	26 71
A system of safeguards for justice was at the heart of the new plan	48	29 73
which said that no one group or person would be in charge and assert one	53	32 76
way over all other ways. Today, we accept this system of checks and	57	34 79
balances. The basis of our union, the constitution, began more than two	62	37 82
hundred years ago. Due to the work of these people who put this nation	67	40 85
and the good of all in front of their own needs, our country did serve	72	43 88
and still serves as an ideal for republics.	74	45 89

HONG KONG

	gwam 3'	5'
Just three years before the twenty-first century will start, the	4	3 50
colony that we have long known as Hong Kong will be finally free from	9	5 52
the hands of the British, who have held power over this place since the	14	8 55
Chinese nation was in control long ago. It is a rock-filled island of	18	11 58
rather small size, not the city as it seems to be on the news. The two	23	14 61
words in the name of the city mean sweet stream and fragrant port.	28	17 64
Those who have been to this area may not have described the city in	32	19 67
these terms, since it is a very active port.	35	21 68
The colony does have one other island and some land on the main-	40	24 71
land. The British have held this land for over a century and a half.	45	27 74
The people per-square-mile is over two-hundred times greater than that	49	30 77
of our nation. Only six of all our states have more people. It has	54	32 80
been agreed by the two nations who will exchange power, that Hong Kong	59	35 82
will still be a free port. There will be freedom of speech, press,	63	38 85
meeting, and travel. The right to strike and to worship will remain.	68	41 88
In the main, the laws will not be changed. It is agreed also that the	73	44 91
island will do its own financial planning and that there will be no new	78	47 94
taxes to pay.	78	47 94

gwam 3' | 1 | 2 | 3 | 4 | 5
5' | 1 | 2 | 3

KEYSTROKING DRILL

Key each line twice; slowly, then faster.

Line: 70 characters
Goal: Key with control; move fingers directly to the punctuation marks without moving hands or arms.

Punctuation Marks

Joe, Mary, and Chung will visit Berlin, Frankfurt, Vienna, and Madrid.
David, the outgoing president, said, "Tonya, Ann, and Al are winners."
There seemed to be much confusion when the young girl screamed "FIRE"!
Are you in town for these holidays: Labor Day, Christmas, and Easter?

The president was motivated by power – – not freedom – – in getting his way.
Course materials included the following: pen, paper, ruler, and tape.
Your self-esteem should give you self-confidence in finishing the job.
Look up these words: (1) catapult, (2) loath, (3) rue, and (4) twill.

Did you read the book review of Treasure Island in the New York Times?
The women's shoes are missing, but the man's ten-speed bike was found.
Ms. Drye spoke on "Ethics"; Mr. Ruiz, on "Taxes"; Mrs. Ames, on "Law."
For breakfast, he ordered ham and eggs, dry toast, danish, and coffee.

	gwam	1'	3'

MARCONI

	gwam	1'	3'
Marconi, inventor of the wireless, or radio, was born midway through	14	5	87
the second half of the nineteenth century. Although he did not attend	28	9	92
a university, he was an avid, self-educated student. His initial labor	42	14	97
was in a foreign country where much experimentation had been done with	57	19	102
a wireless and inventions designed to transmit messages over great dis-	71	24	106
tances. His first successful experiment was to receive a signal eighteen	86	29	111
miles from the point of origin. Shortly thereafter, his ability to	99	33	116
send messages over many miles solicited an invitation from a foreign	113	38	120
newspaper to sponsor wireless experiments on a ship.	123	41	124
The value of the wireless was illustrated when two ships collided.	14	46	128
Because of rapid messages to other ships, there were only three fatali-	28	50	133
ties from one seriously damaged and one sunken ship. Within a few years	42	55	138
following this collision, the Titanic went under. Even though human	56	60	143
loss was very heavy, many survived because wireless communication again	71	65	147
illustrated its contribution to the safety of people in a disaster.	84	69	152
Marconi also worked with microwaves and motion pictures. He predicted	99	74	157
the transmission of a moving picture, which we know today as television.	113	79	162
He died at sixty-one, honored by many nations and societies.	125	83	166

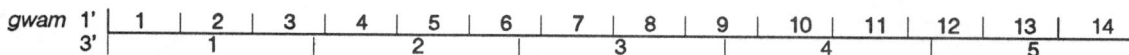

gwam	1'	1	2	3	4	5	6	7	8	9	10	11	12	13	14
	3'		1			2			3			4			5	

PYRAMID PARAGRAPHS

Line: 70 characters
Goal: Build speed. Key each line of paragraph within 15", 12", or 10".

Return with minimum motion; keep eyes on copy.
Key: 1' timing on the paragraph. If you finish a line before the time interval is called, continue to the next line; if not repeat the unfinished line.

	gwam 1'
Steps ought to be taken as	5
soon as possible to reduce the	11
loss that comes from our mass pro-	18
duction and some vexing habits of con-	26
sumption. This great waste is very costly	34
and has a harmful lengthy effect on our lives.	43
We can and must show a great deal more care in the	53
way we spend our scarce resources. We must be able to	64
use and reuse the items which can be salvaged from initial	76
usage. This, of course, is a term very aptly named recycling.	88

gwam 1' | 1 | 2 | 3 | 4 | 5 | 6 | 7 | 8 | 9 | 10 | 11 | 12 | 13 |

---

	gwam 1'	2'	3'
TAXES The government is a firm which is not run with the aim of making a	13	7	4
profit. Its income is based on taxes, which are the payments that by	27	14	9
law we must make to help pay for the cost of our many public services.	42	21	14
Acting alone, none of us would be able to pay for all these services,	56	28	18
but when we as a group share the cost of roads, clean air, schools, the	70	35	23
defense of our nation, public parks, city and state police, and so forth,	85	42	28
we are able to have these and many more benefits in our lives. Most	99	49	33
firms also pay taxes. Taxes are paid on income, payroll, property,	112	56	37
goods and services, imports, gifts, and things that we might inherit.	126	63	42

	gwam 1'	2'	3'
TARIFFS Tariffs are taxes on goods a nation imports. They have been used to	14	7	5
protect local items and to bring in funds for many years. Free trade, a	28	14	9
policy of no tariffs, seems as if it would be a great boon to all as pri-	43	21	14
ces would be less and a better choice could be made. This might be true	56	29	19
in the long run; but in a quick short run, the local job market will see	72	36	24
workers laid off, since the need for local items would go down. Thus,	86	43	29
reduced tariffs are not common in the world today. Yet, nations continue	101	51	34
to work toward a long-range goal of zero tariffs. As the world shrinks,	116	57	39
more and more barriers to free trade will probably be reduced.	128	64	43

gwam 1' | 1 | 2 | 3 | 4 | 5 | 6 | 7 | 8 | 9 | 10 | 11 | 12 | 13 | 14 |
2' | 1 | 2 | 3 | 4 | 5 | 6 | 7 |

CELEBRATING THE NEW YEAR

The beginning of the new year is one of the oldest conventions 4 | 3 | 79
celebrated by mankind. Historically, there have been numerous changes 9 | 5 | 82
relating to the day this ancient festival was celebrated. Some of the 14 | 8 | 85
earliest records indicate it was celebrated when the new moon was near- 18 | 11 | 88
est the spring equinox or, in some cultures, nearest the autumn equinox. 23 | 14 | 91
Caesar is considered responsible for assigning the present date in order 28 | 17 | 94
to venerate a particular deity, Janus. Janus, with one countenance 33 | 20 | 96
looking forward and another looking backward, was the deity of beginnings 38 | 23 | 99
and endings. Some people not only celebrate the new year, they celebrate 43 | 26 | 102
the beginning of every new season. 45 | 27 | 104

The method of celebrating the new year varies extensively from 49 | 29 | 106
country to country. Festivals, among the oldest and most universal of 54 | 32 | 109
celebrations, generally include rituals and ceremonies which express 58 | 35 | 112
mortification, purgation, and jubilation over the renewal of life. For 63 | 38 | 115
many, it is a religious day with attention focused on church activities. 68 | 41 | 118
Many people initiate the new year by emphasizing good conduct on this 73 | 44 | 120
day to increase their bodily and spiritual strength. Their actions 77 | 46 | 123
may take the form of cleaning and purifying their homes or preparing 82 | 49 | 126
a list of imposing resolutions which they hope to keep during the year. 87 | 52 | 129

Customs welcoming the new year often transcend nations, and noise 91 | 55 | 131
is a universal part of the annual festivities. The original purpose of 96 | 57 | 134
a commotion was to frighten away the catastrophic power of any nearby 100 | 60 | 137
demon. Shouting vociferously or banging on a neighbor's door not only 105 | 63 | 140
expressed good sentiments but also drove away demons. Ringing bells at 110 | 66 | 143
the beginning of the new year has always been an international tradition. 115 | 69 | 146
Bells were often covered with heavy material which was gradually removed 120 | 72 | 149
as midnight approached. The clanging increased as material was removed 125 | 75 | 152
until it reached full force promptly at midnight. 128 | 77 | 154

gwam 3' | 1 | 2 | 3 | 4 | 5
5' | 1 | 2 | 3

THE MEANING OF WORK

Most of us work to fulfill a need. To earn money for the basic needs of food, shelter, and clothes is a very crucial need, but this is not always the prime need. Another of our basic needs is to have a feeling of success from doing a job well and to have a feeling that what we are doing is worthwhile. Work is able to bring this satisfaction to many people. In order to be a success in the world of work, we must not only satisfy our employer and ourselves, but we must also meet certain requirements.

A job will require us to work with data, to have insight into people, and to attain some knowledge in our own field of study. To work with data means to be able to handle well many facts, figures, and ideas. To have insight into people demands that we be aware of the needs of others and be able to cope with their problems. To attain knowledge, we must be willing to study hard, keep an open mind, and keep abreast of the recent research done in the field. For most jobs, we need to be capable of doing all three in order to reach success and feel fulfilled.

	3'	5'
	4	3 46
	9	5 48
	13	8 51
	18	11 54
	23	14 57
	27	16 59
	32	19 62
	34	20 63
	38	23 66
	43	26 69
	48	29 72
	52	32 75
	57	34 77
	62	37 80
	66	40 83
	71	43 86

PATIENCE

We long for peace and quiet when we try to perform a task while people move around and make noises and have little thought for us. We may be in haste when people get in our way or delay us in a dozen ways. A word or action, whether meant to cut or not, just may bring us to a boiling point. In these and similar situations, we require forebearance, not just for our sakes but for the benefit of those with whom we come in contact at home, school, or work. What can be done to help us extend our control? To begin, practice patience.

If your patience is tried, look at yourself to see if you are a part of the problem. When in doubt, just assuming the other party is wrong will not show your best patience level. Accept in peace hard words; hold your voice in the face of rudeness. Be ready to hear but slow to talk and slower to anger. Moving too quickly will cause tension and problems; so you must slow down your action and lower your voice. To make it a real test, smile and say a kind word to the person who is getting on your nerves or the one you have been avoiding.

	3'	5'
	4	3 46
	9	5 49
	14	8 52
	18	11 54
	23	14 57
	28	17 60
	33	20 63
	36	22 65
	40	24 68
	45	27 70
	50	30 73
	55	33 76
	60	36 79
	64	39 82
	69	41 85
	72	43 86

gwam 3' | 1 | 2 | 3 | 4 | 5 |
5' | 1 | 2 | 3 |

PYRAMID PARAGRAPHS

Line: 70 characters
Goal: Build speed. Key each line of the paragraph within 15", 12", or 10".

Strike the key with the center of the finger.
Key: 1' timing on the paragraph. If you finish a line before the time interval is called, continue to the next line; if not, repeat the unfinished line.

	gwam 1'
Partnerships are associa-	5
tions of persons (two or more)	11
who agree to go into business for a	18
profit. The agreement need not be writ-	26
ten out. Advantages of a partnership include	35
the fact that more money will be invested and held	45
in reserve than in a single proprietorship. It is also	56
assumed that two or more heads are preferred while operating	68
the firm. However, partners must be congenial and trusting if an	81
enterprise is to furnish an adequate profit and compete in the market.	95

gwam 1' | 1 | 2 | 3 | 4 | 5 | 6 | 7 | 8 | 9 | 10 | 11 | 12 | 13 | 14 |

FINANCIAL STATEMENTS

	gwam 1'	3'
A balance sheet shows the financial status of a company at a precise	14	5	87
time. Assets balance with liabilities and owners' equity. Assets are	28	9	92
the goods and property owned by a company. Liabilities are debts, or	42	14	97
claims against the assets of a company. Owners' equity represents the	56	19	101
balance of assets after the liabilities have been deducted. It includes	71	24	106
the paid-in capital, or investments contributed by stockholders, and the	85	28	111
retained earnings, or the amount that results from profitable operations.	100	33	116
The retained earnings are not distributed to the stockholders but are	114	38	121
kept for expansion and operation of the business.	124	41	124
An income statement is a summary of a company's proceeds and ex-	13	46	128
penses for a definite fiscal period. This document is also known as	27	50	133
an earnings report or a profit-and-loss summary. An income statement	41	55	138
indicates how much money a company gains or loses by comparing earnings	55	60	142
with expenditures. Its elements often encompass sales, cost of sales,	69	64	147
gross profit or loss, selling and administrative costs, depreciation,	83	69	152
operating profit or loss, other income and deductions, earnings or losses	98	74	157
before taxes, provision for taxes, and net earnings or losses. Numerous	113	79	162
ratios can readily be computed from the income statement.	124	83	165

gwam 1' | 1 | 2 | 3 | 4 | 5 | 6 | 7 | 8 | 9 | 10 | 11 | 12 | 13 | 14 |
3' | 1 | | 2 | | 3 | | 4 | | 5 |

KEYSTROKING DRILL

Key the entire drill once; repeat if time permits.   *Line:* 70 characters   *Goal:* Concentrate; space with care; keep fingers curved.

High-Frequency Words

put quite said sale there wall yes you very tax sure such still rest a
unit press plus over own met miles more my net made lot last post only
felt got fit had loss no if for it men nor her oil give old miss death
are clean did eye far fall else cost cut do cent cold at ask go box as
prior met post his four not fit man plus plan up put us to red road by
work able else buy now past last here good has just he only much if in

Low-Frequency Words

opens fox maid keys hare fined ink quit ice ant dome axe horn nut folk
pump harp love fat zip gasp dull dab quest relax fame pop sees bye cue
tab cities grasp lives phone keyed maker takes calm sea soap rasp hack
formal dock taker poke dies dance flue fore sons disc seven ought crab
shift manor push flat robot sox fizz que mass mere stall fad nine teen
arts feed extra port bar reef sizes lox quest noon jolly hum flue sues

---

		gwam	1'	2'	3'

TREES

	1'	2'	3'
The size, form, and rate of growth of trees are all very different.	14	7	5
One type needs almost one hundred years before it is able to reach a	28	14	9
height of ten inches and a diameter of less than one inch. Yet, one of	42	21	14
the big sequoias in the western part of our nation has more than six-	56	28	19
hundred thousand board feet, enough to build forty five-room homes. The	70	35	23
life span of trees is also very different. Some just make it out of the	85	43	28
ground but a certain pine found in the western states may live well	99	49	33
beyond a thousand years.	104	52	35

AUTUMN

	gwam 1'	2'	3'
Autumn is a beautiful time of the year as we see the leaves turn	13	6	4
red, brown, and yellow. It is the choice season for many because the	27	14	9
days for the most part are neither too hot nor too cold. It is an excel-	41	21	14
lent time to take long walks, to crunch the fallen leaves under our feet,	56	28	19
and to view all the wonders of nature. Because of this, many people	70	35	23
like to travel at this time. Fall is a busy season, for various crops	84	42	28
must be harvested and food must be canned and preserved. It is a time	98	49	33
to get into new activities, return to school, and to make new friends.	113	56	38
It is a season during which to begin again, to remember that which has	127	63	42
been, and to appreciate the present.	134	67	45

gwam	1'	1	2	3	4	5	6	7	8	9	10	11	12	13	14
	2'		1		2		3		4		5		6		7

QUARTZ

By studying many chemical analyses, geologists have found that   4 | 3 | 71

silicon and oxygen are the most common elements in the earth's surface.   9 | 5 | 74

These two elements comprise approximately three fourths of the surface   14 | 8 | 77

of the earth. Usually they are united chemically with different elements   19 | 11 | 80

to form large groups of minerals called silicates. Silicon and oxygen   23 | 14 | 83

also may be found alone as mineral quartz. In this mineral, units of   28 | 17 | 86

one silicon atom and two oxygen atoms are repeated millions of times   33 | 20 | 88

in an orderly three-dimensional system. When this internal order is   37 | 22 | 91

reflected externally by an even, flat face in a regular geometric form,   42 | 25 | 94

a crystal results. Various shapes are possible, and crystals usually   47 | 28 | 97

vary from large hexagonal structures that are many feet long to very   51 | 31 | 100

small ones that may be seen only through an electron microscope.   56 | 33 | 102

There are many different varieties of quartz. It appears in water-   60 | 36 | 105

clear crystals or in a large quantity of colors and forms. A pure quartz   65 | 39 | 108

crystal is made of no material except silicon and oxygen and has a trans-   70 | 42 | 111

lucent character. Other varieties may be colored. Many varieties of   75 | 45 | 114

quartz have specific colorations making them valuable for jewelry.   79 | 48 | 116

Amethyst is probably the most outstanding purple variety. Other varie-   84 | 50 | 119

ties include topaz, which is light yellow; rose quartz, which has a   89 | 53 | 122

rose color; and smoky quartz, which is brown or black. Various types   93 | 56 | 125

appear in noncrystal forms, including chalcedony, flint, and jasper.   98 | 59 | 128

A clear red chalcedony is known as carnelian; onyx is generally black   103 | 62 | 130

and white; and several varieties of chalcedony, especially agate, are   107 | 64 | 133

tinted to increase color. Flint is usually gray, brown, or black; and   112 | 67 | 136

jasper is usually red, yellow, or brown.   114 | 69 | 138

gwam 3' | 1 | 2 | 3 | 4 | 5

5' | 1 | 2 | 3

THE NOBEL PRIZE

	gwam 3'	5'
One of the most highly prized awards in the world has the name of	4	3 50
the inventor, Alfred Nobel. This man used his own funds so that awards	9	5 53
can be given each year to men and women who make outstanding contribu-	14	8 56
tions to their areas. The most well-known one is that given to advance	19	11 59
the cause of their field of study. Sweden was the home of this man of	23	14 62
science. He was quite ill much of his life. He had no wife and was	28	17 64
judged to be a cynic by those who knew him. He did not have much educa-	33	20 67
tion, but he did travel often. Due to hard work and study, he knew many	38	23 70
foreign languages and was able to converse easily during his travel	42	25 73
time.	42	25 73
It is odd that a man who was so giving when he set up a program to	47	28 76
further the cause of peace made his fame and money by the making of	51	31 79
explosives. He gave many of these products more power and increased	56	34 81
their use by making them safer to handle. Some say that he believed that	61	37 84
by increasing the power of these devices, the world, in fear, would stop	66	40 87
using them except for peaceful reasons. As we know, this did not take	71	42 90
place. Some also say that the reason for his charity comes from his	75	45 93
great sorrow for the harm done to the world by his inventions.	79	48 95

LEADERSHIP

	gwam 3'	5'
Leadership at its most basic level is the art of getting others to	4	3 45
act. One of the best ways to do this is to give people a chance to be	9	6 48
more responsible in their work. In most cases, workers would like more,	14	8 50
not less, of the action. The more times they are able to contribute,	19	11 53
the more they will feel that what they do really does count. A smart	23	14 56
leader tries to give even those with repetitive jobs a sense of being	28	17 59
involved. He or she can do this by turning over some decisions, by ask-	33	20 62
ing for opinions, and by having workers keep an eye on things at times.	37	23 65
There are many traits that all good leaders have in common. Good	42	25 67
leaders build trust on goodwill rather than on authority. They know the	47	28 70
power of a good example; they are aware that this is one of their best	51	31 73
tools. They know that others see them as they go about their work each	56	34 76
day and that what they do will affect others far more than what they say.	61	37 79
Good leaders have insight into the needs and talents of others. They	66	40 82
note the many good things people do and give credit when it is due.	70	42 84

gwam 3' | 1 | 2 | 3 | 4 | 5 |
5' | 1 | 2 | 3 |

GUIDED WRITING SENTENCES

Line: 70 characters
Goal: Build speed. Key each sentence in 12" or 10".

Key: 30" or 1' timings on the sentences. If you finish a sentence before the time interval is called, go to the next sentence. For each new timing, continue from last complete sentence keyed.

		gwam per line	12"	10"
1	He will collect antiques.		25	30
2	That tree has lost its leaves.		30	36
3	Pay them a just wage for that work.		35	42
4	An attorney is due in court before noon.		40	48
5	Stress your strengths in your critical tasks.		45	52
6	What is as rare as a parking space on a rainy day?		50	60
7	Alarm alone will not restrain rampant pollution habits.		55	66
8	The darker and larger a cloud, the bigger the silver lining.		60	72
9	An ancient map was located in the basement of an apartment house.		65	78
10	The union contract entitles a worker to more than just a minimum wage.		70	84

gwam 1'	1	2	3	4	5	6	7	8	9	10	11	12	13	14
30"	2	4	6	8	10	12	14	16	18	20	22	24	26	28

	gwam	1'	3'

JAPANESE FLOWER ARRANGING

The Japanese art of arranging flowers is called ikebana. It had *(13 | 4 | 86)* its beginning over fourteen hundred years ago in religious devotion to *(27 | 9 | 91)* Buddha. It is said that monks would cut flowers and branches and ar- *(41 | 14 | 96)* range them in tubs on their altars. This ancient art emphasizes form *(55 | 18 | 100)* and balance in linear symmetry according to particular rules resulting *(69 | 23 | 105)* in beautiful and naturally balanced arrangements. Ikebana literally *(83 | 28 | 110)* means the arrangement of living materials in water. It is often de- *(97 | 32 | 114)* scribed as sculpture with flowers. As an avocation, it will not only *(111 | 37 | 119)* capture your imagination and tax your creativity, it will claim your *(124 | 41 | 123)* total personality. *(128 | 43 | 124)*

Color, space, and form are three important features in any floral *(13 | 47 | 129)* arrangement. Ikebana refines our color association by making colors *(27 | 52 | 133)* subordinate to form and using them with restraint. It is the only flo- *(41 | 56 | 138)* ral art that stringently controls use of color and form to create beauti- *(56 | 61 | 143)* ful elegance in the appearance of natural life and growth. One purpose *(70 | 66 | 148)* of ikebana is to make us cooperate closely with nature and instill a *(84 | 71 | 153)* sense of humility, reality, and serenity. Ikebana demands our self- *(97 | 75 | 157)* discipline which, in turn, develops our character. It is a fascinating, *(112 | 80 | 162)* universal, and creative art form. *(119 | 82 | 164)*

gwam 1'	1	2	3	4	5	6	7	8	9	10	11	12	13	14
3'		1		2		3		4		5				

KEYSTROKING DRILL

Key the entire drill twice; repeat if time permits.   *Line:* 70 characters   *Goal:* Key the short words and phrases with continuity.

Space Bar

is no be at hi on as go if nut man fun ago out did this suit cold mind
it is | can be | go to | be in | it will | was in | it was | you can | by the | this was
will not be | one on one | let me know | shall be able | it is not | it has been

so me by it we he of dot put was got sit bird silk hand girl sand quit
what is | can you | why not | put it | must go | now is | not now | there was | can go
it is late | will not be | there is not | hear from you | do not let | why is it

road most crop warm rope coat item drink bound zebra quack elder plant
lack of time | must go now | in the dark | see me soon | will not plan | must go
not in a position | has not been time | what will you do | make up your mind

should thought business computer letter terminal application economics
application letter | computer terminal | economic thought | business systems
key in the letter | turn off the computer | the world of work | read my lips

---

	gwam	1'	2'	3'

LEISURE TIME

The time you are free from work or other duties is leisure time. — 13 | 7 | 4
When you are through with your school work or a job, you may not have — 27 | 14 | 9
much time left. The time left is your free or leisure time. What you do — 42 | 21 | 14
with your free time is a very personal decision. Activities you choose — 56 | 28 | 19
to do during this time should be fun and interesting. If not, you may — 71 | 35 | 23
find life very difficult and boring. Changing your habits can have a — 85 | 42 | 28
good effect on your work. It should be a goal of yours to make life more — 99 | 50 | 33
fun through a variety of activities you select in your free time. There — 114 | 57 | 38
are many things to do with your free time. It might be quite useful, for — 129 | 64 | 43
example, to realize how much time you spend on activities. — 140 | 70 | 47

	gwam	1'	2'	3'

THE JOYS OF FISHING

How can the peace of fishing ever be told? It is a hobby that can — 13 | 6 | 4
offer you a lifetime of pleasure, no matter where you fish or what method — 28 | 14 | 9
you use. It is a sport which has no set rules; there is no time clock — 42 | 21 | 14
to run against; there is no quota to reach. The only condition to be — 56 | 28 | 19
met is a desire for being outside alone with nature and with yourself. — 70 | 35 | 24
Each day is like no other; water, weather, and other conditions are — 84 | 42 | 28
ever changing. The more you fish, the more aware you will become of — 98 | 49 | 33
the habits of fish and the more you will savor the environment. It is — 112 | 56 | 37
said that each day spent fishing is another day added to your life. Do — 127 | 63 | 42
plan to get away for an afternoon and go fishing. — 137 | 68 | 46

gwam	1'	1	2	3	4	5	6	7	8	9	10	11	12	13	14
	2'		1		2		3		4		5		6		7	

SOCCER

Today, there is a possibility that approximately twenty million | 4 | 3 | 87
people play soccer; easily this is the most popular participation sport | 9 | 5 | 90
in the entire world. The game is often referred to as football in more | 14 | 8 | 92
than one hundred and fifty nations where it is commonly played. Amer- | 18 | 11 | 95
ican football, a descendant of soccer, actually places less reliance | 23 | 14 | 98
on the foot than does the precursor. Dimensions of a playing area in | 28 | 17 | 101
soccer are not standardized but certain acceptable minimum parameters | 32 | 19 | 104
have been established beyond which an official field cannot vary. All | 37 | 22 | 106
team participants dress identically except the goalie, who must wear a | 42 | 25 | 109
contrasting color. In addition, the goalie is also the only person who | 46 | 28 | 112
is permitted to touch the ball with the hands; all others utilize the | 51 | 31 | 115
feet, chest, or head. This is an exceptional contest of skill as the | 56 | 33 | 118
feet and head maneuver a ball toward the opposition's goal with short, | 60 | 36 | 120
direct passes from one player to another teammate. Unlike many athletic | 65 | 39 | 123
endeavors, the size of the player is not tantamount to successful per- | 70 | 42 | 126
formance; but agility, speed, coordination, and endurance are represen- | 75 | 45 | 129
tative of other essential requirements. | 77 | 46 | 130

The game has not grown as rapidly as expected in this country; how- | 82 | 49 | 133
ever, an increase in interest in schools has been phenomenal in the past | 87 | 52 | 136
half of the century, considering that five million students now partici- | 91 | 55 | 139
pate. Soccer is the only team sport which conducts a world series or | 96 | 58 | 142
worldwide play-off. Billions now watch the very best of the teams vie | 101 | 60 | 145
for the championship every four years on television. The regulations | 105 | 63 | 147
are relatively simple, and the amount of equipment needed in comparison | 110 | 66 | 150
with other sports justifies its popularity. There is historical sub- | 115 | 69 | 153
stantiation that an athletic event much like soccer was especially pop- | 120 | 72 | 156
ular among the early Greeks and Romans. In professional and amateur | 124 | 75 | 159
contests, one of the major issues has been the rampant enthusiasm, not | 129 | 77 | 161
of players who usually perform in an honorable manner, but fans who have | 134 | 80 | 164
exhibited deplorable behavior at very important national and interna- | 138 | 83 | 167
tional contests. | 140 | 84 | 168

gwam 3' | 1 | 2 | 3 | 4 | 5
5' | 1 | 2 | 3

ARRANGING FLOWERS

Flower arranging is the art of making flowers an artful deco- | 4 | 2 47
ration. One has to consider the shape, the size, and the color. Yet, | 9 | 5 50
the first step when arranging them is to have a design or a basic plan. | 14 | 8 53
It is the design which changes your material from just flowers into a | 18 | 11 56
work of art. Before you begin, decide the height the final design is | 23 | 14 58
to be. There is a simple rule to apply. If the vase is high, the | 27 | 16 61
line from the bottom of the design to the top of the design is two | 32 | 19 64
times the length of the vase. If it is low, the line is the length | 36 | 22 67
plus the width. Once this has been decided, you are ready to start | 41 | 25 69
the design. | 42 | 25 70

Begin by cutting the first flower as high as you would like your | 46 | 28 72
design to be and place it in the center of the vase. Prepare your next | 51 | 30 75
flower so that it will be two-thirds as high as the first one and cut | 55 | 33 78
another to be one-third as high as the first one. Arrange the second | 60 | 36 81
flower slightly in front and to the right of the first flower. Place | 65 | 39 84
the third flower to the left of center directly in line with the second | 70 | 42 86
one. The product is a triangle, an important and basic line of a design. | 74 | 45 89

JOB SEARCHING

Most people do not know what jobs are available to them now or may | 4 | 3 44
become open in the near future. Taking a job too soon may mean that one | 9 | 6 47
misses the chance to find a better job. If a person knew all of the | 14 | 8 50
vacant jobs that were open to that person, there would be no need to | 18 | 11 53
search. The person with a job could then transfer to a new and better | 23 | 14 56
job without first planning a job search. Unfortunately, most people do | 28 | 17 59
not have complete data about jobs before they begin to hunt for them. | 33 | 20 61

Since most people do not know the unfilled jobs for which they | 37 | 22 64
are qualified, they must take much time reading ads, making calls, and | 42 | 25 67
setting up interviews. The collecting of this data is a great expense | 46 | 28 70
in terms of money as well as time. The longer one may try to find a job, | 51 | 31 73
the greater the cost may be. The longer one takes to find a job, the | 56 | 34 75
greater also may be the benefits in the form of finding a better job | 61 | 36 78
with higher pay. We realize that people will look at these costs and | 65 | 39 81
benefits when they decide on the amount of time to look for a job. | 70 | 42 84

gwam 3' | 1 | 2 | 3 | 4 | 5
5' | 1 | 2 | 3

KEYSTROKING DRILL

Key each line once with steady stroking, complete control. Repeat each line at a higher rate but still with control.

Concentrate as you key.
Line: 70 characters

Goal: Preview of intricate words in the next seven timings.

Difficult Words

ox, accessories, andirons, synthetic, elaborate, monoxide, utilitarian environmental, distracting, excessive, acoustically, absorbent, design

tantamount, agility, endeavor, maneuver, utilize, endurance, precursor ikebana, religious, symmetry, emphasizes, deviation, linear, sculpture

hexagonal, silicates, quartz, colorations, chalcedony, onyx, amethysts investments, profitable, deductions, depreciation, ratios, expenditure

historically, festival, equinox, catastrophic, clanging, deity, demons purgation, mortification, liabilities, chemical, geologist, pleasanter

oxygen, electron, jasper, avocation, stringently, humility, atmosphere phenomenal, substantiation, fascinating, vehicles, descendant, scrawls

silicon, serenity, bellows, parameters, creativity, carbon, microscope pollution, progressively, utilized, dimensions, purifying, countenance

		gwam	1'	3'
REDUCING OFFICE NOISE	Noise is a serious environmental factor in any office, particularly	14	5	58
	in word processing areas because of noisy printers. Distracting and	27	9	62
	excessive noise can lower morale, lower productivity, reduce decision-	41	14	67
	making ability, and become a risk to one's health. Companies can con-	55	18	71
	trol noise in many ways when planning and designing offices. Separate	70	23	76
	work stations with panels that have been acoustically treated to absorb	84	28	81
	sound can be designed; ceilings can be made with material which is tex-	98	33	86
	tured and sound absorbent; carpeting with padding made of material that	113	38	91
	allows air to circulate through it, thus absorbing sound, can be used;	127	42	95
	and printers can be covered with acoustical hoods. Any of these acous-	141	47	100
	tical treatments will lower the noise level in an office and help assure	156	52	105
	a pleasanter work area.	160	53	106

		gwam	1'	3'
THE FIREPLACE	From even the earliest times, the fireplace was utilized as a prin-	13	4	54
	cipal source of heat, as an origin for inside light, and as a means for	28	9	59
	cooking or preparing food. The size of fireplaces ranged from extremely	42	14	64
	small to large enough to cook an ox. Elaborate but seldom used conveni-	57	19	69
	ence accessories, such as andirons, synthetic firewood, and bellows, are	71	24	74
	absolutely necessary today because the fireplace has become a decorative	86	29	78
	object. It is not the energy source of earlier times. However, a change	101	34	83
	to a nonutilitarian activity can probably be justified, since fewer	114	38	88
	fireplace fires will mean less carbon monoxide going into the atmosphere.	129	43	93
	Fortunately, there will be progressively more quality air; and we will	144	48	98
	experience reduced pollution.	149	50	100

gwam 1' | 1 | 2 | 3 | 4 | 5 | 6 | 7 | 8 | 9 | 10 | 11 | 12 | 13 | 14 |
3' | 1 | 2 | 3 | 4 | 5 |

GUIDED WRITING SENTENCES

Line: 60 characters
Goal: Build speed. Key each sentence in 12" or 10".

Key: 30" or 1' timings on the sentences. If you finish a sentence before the time interval is called, go to the next sentence. For each new timing, continue from last complete sentence keyed.

		gwam per line	12"	10"
1	You were wrong about the size.		30	36
2	The idea seems to be a good one.		32	38
3	The fact is that you are too slow.		34	41
4	We shall let you know in a few days.		36	43
5	We carry your size at the other store.		38	46
6	In any case, your reason is quite clear.		40	48
7	The book was checked out for three months.		42	50
8	We are very sorry that we cannot assist you.		44	53
9	Your payment will be sent to you on the first.		46	55
10	Plan to visit us in our new building next month.		48	58
11	The purpose of the drive will be explained to you.		50	60
12	You should receive the supply within the next month.		52	62

gwam	1'	1	2	3	4	5	6	7	8	9	10
	30"	2	4	6	8	10	12	14	16	18	20

		gwam 1'	2'	3'

TORTS

A tort is an act that is wrong which might result in injury to / 13 / 6 / 4
a person or in property loss to that person. It might not be recognized / 27 / 14 / 9
as a crime. An act against the person is known as a tort, while a crime / 42 / 21 / 14
is an act against the state. Quite often a wrong act is a tort and a / 56 / 28 / 19
crime, since it is both an act against the person and the state. The / 70 / 35 / 23
person who executed an act that is a tort and a crime is subject to a / 84 / 42 / 28
civil lawsuit and prosecution. People must account for their actions. / 98 / 49 / 32
When people direct their children to take part in an act or do not take / 113 / 56 / 37
action to stop the act, they might be held responsible. Therefore, take / 127 / 63 / 42
care about what you say, write, or do to another person. / 138 / 69 / 46

		gwam 1'	2'	3'

LEARNING TO DISAGREE

One secret of getting along well with other people is to learn to / 13 / 7 / 4
disagree without being disagreeable. Use tact when you do not agree. / 27 / 14 / 9
You begin to mature when you are content to know that you are right / 41 / 20 / 14
about a point without the need to show that the other person is wrong. / 55 / 28 / 18
Often one of the best ways to let people know that they are wrong is to / 70 / 35 / 23
let them have their own way. In a social circumstance, do not dispute / 84 / 42 / 28
with others even if you know they are wrong. Do not argue about facts; / 98 / 49 / 33
be more interested in where the conversation is headed rather than if / 112 / 56 / 37
you win or lose an argument. It is not what we say or do but how we / 126 / 63 / 42
speak or act that determines how well we are accepted. / 137 / 68 / 46

gwam	1'	1	2	3	4	5	6	7	8	9	10	11	12	13	14
	2'		1		2		3		4		5		6		7

GENEALOGY

| | 4 | 3 | 84 |
Genealogy is the study of family descent. Introduced another way,

it is a diagram of recorded history of the lineage of a person or family | 9 | 6 | 87 |

from an ancestor or ancestors. The examination allows one to look back | 14 | 8 | 89 |

to visualize his or her forbearers; how and where they lived; and who | 19 | 11 | 92 |

their siblings, parents, and grandparents were. Each of us has some | 23 | 14 | 95 |

interest in history. What famous past major events could be associated | 28 | 17 | 98 |

with our family? Genealogy has been recognized as a quality science for | 33 | 20 | 101 |

many centuries. Royal families and their adherents believe it is needed | 38 | 23 | 104 |

because they assign much importance to making certain that precise blood | 43 | 26 | 107 |

lines are transmitted to rightful beneficiaries and that nobility is | 47 | 28 | 109 |

maintained. There are also countless biblical references to family | 52 | 31 | 112 |

lineage. | 52 | 31 | 112 |

The sources often used in a lineage search are family bibles and | 57 | 34 | 115 |

albums, church reviews, census reports, federal and state statistics and | 62 | 37 | 118 |

licenses, military documents, old papers, markers in cemeteries, and many | 67 | 40 | 121 |

others. Librarians, some with a speciality in clan studies, can assist | 71 | 43 | 124 |

and save the searcher much time and energy. Organizations with an em- | 76 | 46 | 127 |

phasis in genealogy may be joined to aid the searcher and provide an | 81 | 48 | 129 |

interface with others interested in the same undertaking. There are | 85 | 51 | 132 |

also family units organized to assist all those with the identical last | 90 | 54 | 135 |

name to conduct a search and explore possible relationships. | 94 | 56 | 137 |

At some future time, the wizardry of data storage and immediate | 98 | 59 | 140 |

retrieval will allow family members to simply depress keys to call up | 103 | 62 | 143 |

information on an ancestor in a matter of seconds. This will be the | 108 | 65 | 145 |

supreme sensation for one interested in genealogy. However, initially | 112 | 67 | 148 |

the information must be located, cataloged, verified, and stored. To | 117 | 70 | 151 |

the true scholar of genealogy, the reward will not be in depressing the | 122 | 73 | 154 |

precise keys to obtain the information but in the satisfaction that comes | 127 | 76 | 157 |

from completing quiet, painstaking research that was needed to locate, | 131 | 79 | 160 |

examine, assemble, confirm, and journalize the data. | 135 | 81 | 162 |

gwam 3' | 1 | 2 | 3 | 4 | 5 |
5' | 1 | 2 | 3 |

COMPETITION

	gwam	3'	5'

As a consumer, you have a big choice as to what you will buy. Most | 4 | 3 | 51
of the time, you are able to choose from whom you will buy. For example, | 9 | 6 | 54
suppose that two or more companies each sell their own quality of paper. | 14 | 9 | 57
Each firm will try to get you to buy its own paper. When you have two | 19 | 11 | 60
or more firms that try to sell to the same people, this is called compe- | 24 | 14 | 62
tition. Competition exists among firms to sell their goods and services. | 29 | 17 | 65
It may also be present among people who try to sell their skills and | 33 | 20 | 68
talents. | 34 | 20 | 68

When there are many sellers of the same product, you will have | 38 | 23 | 71
perfect competition. In some parts of our economy, competition is far | 43 | 26 | 74
from perfect. In fact, in some segments, there may be little or no | 47 | 28 | 76
choice. A case in which there is just one seller of a good or service | 52 | 31 | 79
is a monopoly. You must recognize that when this case exists, you have | 57 | 34 | 82
no choice as to where to shop. You must buy from that firm or you do not | 62 | 37 | 85
buy at all. The water company is a good example. In your town, is | 67 | 40 | 88
there more than one firm that gives this basic service? Do you have a | 71 | 43 | 91
choice when you buy electrical service? Most people now agree that they | 76 | 46 | 94
want to have a choice when they buy a product or service. | 80 | 48 | 96

STOP PAYMENT ORDER

	gwam	3'	5'

More bills are paid by check than by cash. One of the key ad- | 4 | 2 | 46
vantages of using a checking account is that checks are safer to carry | 9 | 5 | 49
and use than money. When a check is lost or stolen, it is easier to | 13 | 8 | 51
replace than currency. You do not expect to lose a check; but when you | 18 | 11 | 54
do realize that a check has been lost, a stop-payment order should be | 23 | 14 | 57
placed at once. A stop-payment order is a form that asks your bank not | 28 | 17 | 60
to pay a specified check that you have written. You are just telling | 32 | 19 | 63
the bank that the check was lost or stolen. | 35 | 21 | 65

You must visit the bank to sign the stop-payment order. As you | 39 | 24 | 67
complete the form, you need to know the check number, the name of the | 44 | 26 | 70
person or firm to whom the check is made payable, and the exact amount. | 49 | 29 | 73
The check's date is also important. You will be asked why you wish to | 54 | 32 | 76
stop payment on the check. The form is then processed by the bank. | 58 | 35 | 78
When the check is presented for payment by the payee, the bank will | 63 | 38 | 81
refuse to pay the check. The bank will return the check to the person | 68 | 41 | 84
presenting it for payment. A nominal fee is charged for this service. | 72 | 43 | 87

| gwam 3' | 1 | 2 | 3 | 4 | 5 |
| 5' | 1 | | 2 | | 3 |

PYRAMID PARAGRAPHS

Line: 70 characters
Goal: Build speed. Key each line of the paragraph within 15", 12", or 10".

Use a light, confident touch.
Key: 1' timing on the paragraph. If you finish a line before the time

interval is called, continue to the next line; if not, repeat the unfinished line.

	gwam 1'
The United States had few	
taxes in its earliest history.	5
Initially, the country received its	11
support by internal taxes on sugar, sale	18
by auction, and spirits. Later, wars as well	26
as similar demands created the need for additional	35
money, so sales taxes were put on gold and silver. Our	45
first income tax came during the Civil War but stopped a few	56
decades later when declared unconstitutional. A turnabout was to	68
come, the Sixteenth Amendment. We have had income taxes to pay since.	81

gwam 1' | 1 | 2 | 3 | 4 | 5 | 6 | 7 | 8 | 9 | 10 | 11 | 12 | 13 | 14 |

---

	gwam 1'	3'
GOLF Golf appears in many ways to be a paradoxical sport. Golfers vigor-	14	5	57

GOLF

	gwam 1'	3'
Golf appears in many ways to be a paradoxical sport. Golfers vigor-	14	5 / 57
ously hit the ball, only to go chasing after it. They talk about getting	28	9 / 61
necessary exercise; however, they purchase electric carts to minimize	42	14 / 66
walking. Sand hazards and artificial bodies of water are added to the	57	19 / 71
course to make it both interesting and frustrating. To further challenge	71	24 / 76
players, the grass is cut either high or low in particular areas. A new	86	29 / 81
vocabulary including words like birdie, bogey, handicap, and eagle must	100	33 / 85
be assimilated. Golfers practice endlessly so that they won't have to	115	38 / 90
hit the ball so often; oddly enough, the individual receiving the low	128	43 / 95
score is victorious. However, despite all of these challenges, more	143	48 / 100
individuals are attracted to and become supporters of golf every year.	157	52 / 104

APRICOTS

	gwam 1'	3'
China is generally considered to be the original home of the apri-	13	4 / 56
cot. History informs us that philosophers found the fruit and shade of	28	9 / 61
the apricot tree inspiring and that they therefore did much of their	41	14 / 66
meditating and deliberating under these trees. Apricots were also once	56	19 / 71
thought to have extraordinary health-giving powers. Today apricots are	70	23 / 75
cultivated all over the world. In this country, production is restricted	85	28 / 80
to areas where the climatic conditions are favorable. Although most va-	99	33 / 85
rieties can withstand the winter cold, the fruit blossoms early and is	114	38 / 90
susceptible to late freezes. Apricots provide a considerable amount of	128	43 / 95
iron in addition to two necessary vitamins. This healthful delicacy can	143	48 / 100
be preserved by canning or drying and is excellent when used in desserts.	157	52 / 104

gwam 1' | 1 | 2 | 3 | 4 | 5 | 6 | 7 | 8 | 9 | 10 | 11 | 12 | 13 | 14 |
3' | 1 | 2 | 3 | 4 | 5 |

PYRAMID PARAGRAPHS

Line: 70 characters
Goal: Build speed. Key each line of the paragraph within 15", 12", or 10".

Break through your speed ceiling.
Key: 1' timing on the paragraph. If you finish a line before the time interval is called, continue to the next line; if not, repeat the unfinished line.

	gwam 1'
Have you ever thought of	
operating your own business?	5
People go into business for many	11
reasons. Many of these reasons seem	17
to be common among business owners. Few	24
people will say their primary reason for go-	32
ing into business was to make money; most of the	41
others often state that they had a desire to develop	51
a large company. The reasons continue on and on. There	61
are several advantages for going into business for yourself.	72
	84

gwam 1' | 1 | 2 | 3 | 4 | 5 | 6 | 7 | 8 | 9 | 10 | 11 | 12 |

		gwam 1'	2'	3'
ORNITHOLOGY	The study of birds is known as ornithology. This is a very serious	14	7	4
	field of study for many people. Scientists band birds or place radio	28	14	9
	transmitters on them so they may note the rules of travel and learn how	42	21	14
	long they live and where they live. Most types of birds are known at	56	28	19
	this time except for a few classes in remote areas of the world. To	70	35	23
	many other people, looking at birds is just a hobby. There are many	84	42	28
	facts about birds that interest us, such as their pretty color, their	98	49	33
	songs, and their way of life. Many keep a list of the birds they see	112	56	37
	and note items of interest, some make a new list each year, and some	126	69	42
	make a life-long list to go with this intriguing life-long study.	139	69	46

		gwam 1'	2'	3'
OUR CONSTITUTION	The constitution of our nation is the basic law of our land. All	13	7	4
	other laws in the land must follow it. It gives powers and rights to	27	13	9
	the government as well as limits them. It also defines the rights of	41	20	14
	citizens. It tells public officials what they can and cannot do. If	55	28	18
	an official interferes with the rights of a person, that person can go	69	35	23
	to court and force the official to stop violating the law. Before our	84	42	28
	constitution became the law of the land, it had to have the approval of	98	49	33
	the people in each of the states. Now, if at any time there is to be a	112	56	37
	change in this law, it is done by an amendment which must be approved	126	64	42
	by the people. Very few changes have been made in this law since it	140	70	47
	was first passed years ago. Each state also has its own constitution.	154	77	51

gwam 1' | 1 | 2 | 3 | 4 | 5 | 6 | 7 | 8 | 9 | 10 | 11 | 12 | 13 | 14 |
2' | 1 | 2 | 3 | 4 | 5 | 6 | 7 |

PETROLEUM

	gwam 3'	5'
Oil is thought to be a bane or a necessary evil since this valuable	4	3 47
resource is so much in demand. It makes the headlines as a cause of war,	9	6 50
an example of monopoly, and a leading cause of environmental problems.	14	9 52
It is a valuable raw material and access seems to be a requirement if a	19	11 55
society wishes a higher standard of living. Petroleum is needed to	24	14 58
lubricate machines and provide fuel for all types of vehicles and for	28	17 61
heating and cooling. This item is a raw material that is required in	33	20 64
paints, cosmetics, medicines, rubber, solvents, cleaners, soaps, candy,	38	23 66
waxes, and chewing gum. With so many major uses, it would be difficult	43	25 69
if not impossible to stop importing billions of dollars' worth per year.	47	28 72
Unfortunately, it is not easily accessible; it is costly and dangerous,	52	31 75
and it creates problems of pollution. As more nations become industri-	57	34 78
alized requiring energy, the competition for petroleum increases. We can,	62	37 81
however, become better consumers by recycling, using substitutes, and	67	40 84
developing an attitude that is consumer-centered instead of extravagant,	72	43 87
conspicuous consumption.	73	44 88

GRAFFITI

	gwam 3'	5'
Graffito is a general term for a casual writing or drawing on an	4	3 45
ancient building, cavern, or other such surface. Today many people refer	9	6 48
to these writings by the plural form of the word, graffiti. Early graf-	14	8 50
fiti were evidently written or drawn with a sharp object or with char-	19	11 53
coal. Graffiti are significant to linguists for the information they	23	14 56
furnish about the spoken language of the period during which they were	28	17 59
written. They are also extremely valuable to historians for the inti-	33	20 62
mate details they reveal concerning the customs of ordinary citizens.	37	22 64
Today satirical graffiti can be seen in many public places, such as	42	25 67
on vending machines, subway walls, fences, and billboards. Amazingly,	46	28 70
it is rare that anyone is actually seen doing the writing. Modern graf-	51	31 73
fiti are often so witty and so cleverly done that experienced writers	56	34 76
frequently copy the ideas for their own materials. Professionals do not	61	37 79
agree as to why people scrawl graffiti. However, this ancient custom	65	39 81
will probably always be followed by people who wish to convey messages.	70	42 84

```
gwam 3' |        1        |        2        |        3        |        4        |        5        |
     5' |             1             |             2             |             3             |
```

		gwam	3'	5'

GROUP HEALTH INSURANCE

As you begin to earn an income, you will realize that you must become concerned with your health. This concern should focus on how you can maintain good health as well as what you must do to protect it. How do you go about obtaining health insurance? Your best buy is to join a group health plan if you can. Often, you do not need a physical examination to join. You should join during the enrollment periods open to you. If you work for a firm that has a group plan, you may be required to join the plan soon after you start work. If you do not, you may have to wait up to a year for the next enrollment period.

gwam 3'	5'
4	2 47
9	5 49
14	8 52
19	11 55
24	14 58
28	17 61
33	20 64
38	23 67
41	25 69

You can expect to pay a low fee through a firm. Your firm may pay part or all of the cost of the insurance for you. As a member in the group plan, you will get a brochure that describes the benefits. In most cases, you may convert to individual health insurance when you leave a firm. There are many good group health plans. You may elect a plan which covers the cost of all needed services rather than one that sets limits in dollars. So the first step is to check the limits.

46	27 71
50	30 74
55	33 77
60	36 80
65	39 83
69	42 86
73	44 88

gwam 3'	5'

WRITING BUSINESS LETTERS

A business letter is one of the most common ways to send a message to someone. When you start a new job, you will be asked to write letters. However, you may not begin writing letters during the first week. After being on the job for a few weeks or months, let your boss know that you have a skill for writing letters. He or she may like a chance to observe what you can do. From time to time, attempt answering a letter that has just arrived in the incoming mail. Place it on the boss's desk. As you are asked to compose more letters, realize you are increasing your value to the firm.

4	3 45
9	5 47
14	8 50
19	11 53
24	14 56
28	17 59
33	20 62
38	23 65
40	24 66

Writing a business letter is a hard task. A letter that goes out has a special job to do. Try to keep in mind that the reader must understand and respond to the message. You must know how to express yourself well in a letter so that the meaning will be clear. As you write a letter, question whether or not the letter will get results. Make getting results your goal. The more letters you write, the easier it will be for you to reach this goal.

44	26 68
49	29 71
54	32 74
58	35 77
63	38 80
68	41 83
70	42 84

gwam 3'	1	2	3	4	5
5'	1		2		3

GUIDED WRITING SENTENCES

Line: 70 characters
Goal: Build speed. Key each sentence in 12" or 10".

Key: 30" or 1' timings on the sentences. If you finish a sentence before the time interval is called, go to the next sentence. For each new timing, continue from last complete sentence keyed.

		gwam per line	12"	10"
1	The auditor signed today.		25	30
2	Please chair the sports panel.		30	36
3	Estate taxes should not be ignored.		35	42
4	A good reporter will never editorialize.		40	48
5	The ancient map gave no clues as to the mine.		45	52
6	Confucius was a teacher, a statesman, and a leader.		50	60
7	Their underground water supply continues to be reduced.		55	66
8	In most cases, the data sheet should be limited to one page.		60	72
9	Hazardous waste was an unrecognized problem for a very long time.		65	78
10	She believed that the minimum wage would hurt more than it would help.		70	84

gwam 1'	1	2	3	4	5	6	7	8	9	10	11	12	13	14
30"	2	4	6	8	10	12	14	16	18	20	22	24	26	28

---

		gwam	1'	3'

TRADEMARKS

	gwam	1'	3'
Firms often create brand names, or trademarks, to identify their	13	4	56
products or services and to distinguish them from the goods of competi-	27	9	61
tors. A trademark may be a word, a design, a label, or some other sym-	41	14	66
bol. Trademarks are frequently seen in advertising and are important	55	18	70
guides for consumers. Individuals who have utilized a particular article	70	23	75
once can purchase the identical brand again with some assurance of re-	84	28	80
ceiving an article of a similar quality. Furthermore, manufacturers who	99	33	85
advertise regularly with the idea of establishing a reputation for their	113	38	90
brands try to maintain a very high standard of quality. Therefore, their	128	43	95
goods tend to be more reliable than those of other producers. Firms can	143	48	100
protect their trademarks by registering them with the government.	156	52	104

DICTION

	gwam	1'	3'
Unfortunately, very few of us realize the importance of proper	13	4	56
diction today. Diction refers to selection of words, manner of speak-	27	9	61
ing, and enunciation. We are very lazy. We slur short and long words,	41	14	65
use verbiage and jargon without any reason, and carelessly omit sylla-	55	18	70
bles and suffixes. Just listen attentively and you can hear mumbles,	69	23	75
grunts, and honks instead of clear, concise, beautiful language. Your	83	28	80
responsibility in labor and in living requires that you always be under-	98	32	84
stood, that you talk forcefully and with meaning. A voice and vocabulary	112	37	89
will be analyzed as much as a physical appearance in an interview. Do	127	42	94
not exasperate listeners by mutilating the vernacular. Major advantages	141	47	99
will be yours if your language is correct, is clear, and is appropriate.	156	52	104

gwam 1'	1	2	3	4	5	6	7	8	9	10	11	12	13	14
3'		1		2		3		4		5				

KEYSTROKING DRILL

Key the entire drill; repeat if time permits.   *Line:* 70 characters   *Goal:* Key at a steady pace with hand and arms motionless; stress control.

Left-Hand Words

great refer fever grate draft verge staff greet after tract abate verb
defeat effect career target freeze excess secret create severe creased
axes sets stew waxed brass swabs sewed vexes assessed grasses stresses

area fax data afar razz czar zag raze saga zest agate daze award craze
verb extra weave trade water tweed dwarf exact craft fewer brace badge
agree beard serve facet watts scare vertex estate zagged facade vacate

Right-Hand Words

him null upon monk join jumpy minimum homonym unholy nonunion monopoly
kin pink mink link milk kill kiln kink junk kimono kinky minion pompon ill oil
poll only look polo pool polk null jolly loony million opinion

up pip pulp pupil poppy nippy plump puppy pippin pompon poplin pumpkin
polo kill lull punk milk oily poll noon join hymn noun mink monk imply
poplin million minimum lollipop nonunion uphill unhook kimono monopoly

	gwam	1'	2'	3'

INVESTING YOUR SAVINGS

	1'	2'	3'
An investment may take the form of a piece of land, a work of art,	13	7	4
a bond, stock, or cash in a savings account. All of these change in	27	13	9
value and will earn you money, but some more quickly than others. Before	42	21	14
making an investment of any kind, ask yourself how vital such things as	56	28	19
safety, liquidity, and rate of return are to you. If you have only a	70	35	23
small amount of money to invest, you should look for a very safe invest-	85	42	28
ment. You may also want one that is liquid, or one which can be turned	99	49	33
into money very fast. Cash and savings in a bank are very liquid, but	113	57	38
art may not be. You may also want an investment that has a high rate	127	64	42
of return; however, a high rate of return means the risk will be great.	142	71	47
Investments demand careful planning before you choose.	153	76	51

gwam 1' 2' 3'

FASHION

	1'	2'	3'
Fashion is a complex term. In the study of fashion today, quite a	13	7	4
few words are used over and over again, such as style, design, high	27	13	9
fashion, and taste. The meanings of these terms must be known so that we	42	21	14
can understand the concepts of fashion. A style that is recognized and	56	28	19
used by a group at any one time, no matter how small that group, is a	70	35	23
fashion. A design is a special part of a style. High fashion means a	84	42	28
style or design selected by a small group of leaders who are first to	98	49	33
accept the new fashion. Taste is the opinion of what is and what is not	113	56	38
fit for a given place. Just about all that we do in our daily life is	127	64	42
affected by these fashions, which are a big business today.	139	69	46

gwam	1'	1	2	3	4	5	6	7	8	9	10	11	12	13	14
	2'		1		2		3		4		5		6		7	

| | gwam | 3' | 5' |

METHANOL

Methanol is a clear, colorless, volatile, inflammable, poisonous liquid or gas which can cause death or blindness. In addition, this gas is also dangerous if inhaled or if it comes into contact with the epidermis. Methanol is not located in a natural state but is a product of organic materials such as coal, wood, agricultural commodities, and garbage. It is sometimes called wood alcohol although this will refer only to methanol that is a final product made through a destructive wood distillation process. This liquid is necessary in making plastics, antifreeze, solvents, and rocket fuel. But the major possibility for this malevolent-sounding liquid is as a substitute for gasoline in motor vehicles as its combustion will not pollute the environment. Thus far, the expense of processing a trouble-free motor fuel has been prohibitive; but gasohol, the combining of methanol and gasoline, has been successful. As the number of cars and expense of petroleum-based gasoline increases, this dangerous-sounding product may become safer and become the necessary energy source of the future.

gwam (3')	3'	5'
4	3	47
9	5	50
14	8	53
19	11	55
23	14	58
28	17	61
33	20	64
38	23	67
42	25	70
47	28	72
51	31	75
56	34	78
61	37	81
66	39	83
70	42	86
73	44	88

| | gwam | 3' | 5' |

ACUPUNCTURE

Acupuncture is an ancient Chinese method of treatment or remedy to ease pain. Needles of excellent quality are inserted into the spinal cord or into other areas to make contact with nerve endings. This art has been an established practice in the Orient for numerous centuries. The geographical regions in which heavy usage has generally occurred are those where a medical program, hospital, doctor, or other healing personnel are in short supply.

Much acupuncture interest has arisen worldwide in recent decades. This is probably due to its success in the Orient and positive publicity on the extensive use and virtue of the treatment. The acceptance is also due to having more trained personnel who offer acupuncture services to the public and recognition by medical insurance, as well as grudging acceptance from some medical practitioners. In addition, many people have lost their fear by realizing that a needle must not always be painful. Despite the lack of universal recognition, it appears that acupuncture has earned a justified position as a supplement to accompany more widely accepted medical practices.

gwam (3')	3'	5'
4	3	48
9	5	50
14	8	53
19	11	56
23	14	59
28	17	62
30	18	63
34	21	66
39	24	69
44	26	71
49	29	74
54	32	77
58	35	80
63	38	83
68	41	86
73	44	89
75	45	90

gwam 3' | 1 | 2 | 3 | 4 | 5
5' | 1 | 2 | 3

BIRD WATCHING

	gwam	3'	5'
You have been seeing birds as far back as you can remember, and you	4	3	81
will continue seeing them wherever you may be. It is a real pleasure to	9	6	84
see them. You can see more kinds of birds by learning how to look for	14	8	87
them and at them. You should begin by giving your attention to the birds	19	11	90
in your own community. You expect to learn these first. Do not try to	24	14	93
learn the details of size, shape, or color of head or tail. Learn to	28	17	96
know the whole bird as one total picture, since one quick look at a	33	20	98
moving bird may be all you will get. When you can recognize a cardinal	38	23	101
or a magpie, then look mainly at the details that make it stand out.	42	25	104
You will find more people who are interested in birds than you	47	28	106
can imagine. Often, they are in a type of club. Some people just get	51	31	109
together and look for birds. They like to share what they know with	56	34	112
you. If you are beginning, remember that everyone was once a beginner.	61	36	115
If you want to learn about birds, ask questions. Before you know it,	65	39	118
people will be coming to you with their questions. Go look for birds	70	42	121
when you can. The best time of the day is in the early morning. By the	75	45	123
time the sun is well up, bird activity is reduced, and it does not	80	48	126
increase until late in the afternoon. Try to get out early on a spring	84	51	129
morning when most of the birds are migrating north.	88	53	131
No special equipment is needed for seeing birds, just good eyes.	92	55	134
Good ears are a help, too. Yet, there are ways of increasing your	97	58	137
sightings at a low cost. Field glasses are the most important item of	101	61	139
equipment. A good pair of glasses is a fine tool and should be selected	106	64	142
with care. The best ones are made with prisms to keep their size small.	111	67	145
They should have a single control to make them easy to use. The power of	116	70	148
the glass will indicate how much larger it makes a bird appear. Take	121	72	151
your time when you plan to buy, since this may be an investment for life.	126	75	154
Why not start to watch birds now? You will learn much, and you will like	131	78	157
it.	131	79	157

gwam 3' | 1 | 2 | 3 | 4 | 5
5' | 1 | 2 | 3

PART 3

DIFFICULT COPY

Part 3 includes speed-building and technique drills as well as keystroking drills which preview the difficult words found in the timed writings in this Part. Goals for each drill are included.

Part 3 includes 1', 3', and 5' triple-controlled timed writings of difficult copy (syllable intensity, 1.83; average word length, 6.3; high-frequency words, 70%). Copy in script and rough draft is also presented.

KEYSTROKING DRILL

Key each line once with steady stroking, complete control. Repeat each line at a higher rate but still with control.

Concentrate as you key.
Line: 70 characters

Goal: Preview of intricate words in the next ten timings.

Difficult Words

innovation, actualized, optic, communication, astound, experimentation
grudging, practitioners, acupuncture, geographical, universal, medical

volatile, poisonous, malevolent, epidermis, agricultural, distillation
enunciation, verbiage, vernacular, mutilating, exasperate, attentively

manufacturers, distinguish, trademarks, symbol, individuals, assurance
graffito, linguist, intimate, historian, satirical, billboards, subway

industrialized, resource, monopoly, environmental, petroleum, cosmetic
frustrated, paradoxical, vigorously, assimilated, minimize, artificial

philosophers, inspiring, delicacy, susceptible, deliberating, climatic
descent, lineage, genealogy, interface, ancestor, siblings, cemeteries

forebearers, vitamins, handicap, solvents, waxes, cleverly, meditating
analyzed, forcefully, prohibitive, worldwide, converted, relationships

---

	gwam	1'	3'
TELEPHONE INNOVATIONS The information age is upon us and progress in communication is	13	4	50
continuing to astound us. Telephones are increasing their capacity with	27	9	54
the use of fiber optic cables. Instead of just dialing someone, callers	42	14	59
will be able to transmit photographs and reports. A sharp quality pic-	56	19	64
ture will be projected thousands of miles over the wires. Written mes-	70	23	69
sages can and will be converted into voice and delivered over cellular	85	28	74
phones. A wide variety of cultural materials will be distributed to	98	33	78
people via telephone systems. Small telephones will be carried in a	112	37	83
pocket. Many similar innovations are under experimentation now, but	126	42	87
they will be actualized and expanded in the future.	136	45	91

gwam 1' | 1 | 2 | 3 | 4 | 5 | 6 | 7 | 8 | 9 | 10 | 11 | 12 | 13 | 14 |
3' | 1 | 2 | 3 | 4 | 5 |

GUIDED WRITING SENTENCES

Line: 60 characters
Goal: Build speed. Key each sentence in 12" or 10".

Key: 30" or 1' timings on the sentences. If you finish a sentence before the time interval is called, go to the next sentence. For each new timing, continue from last complete sentence keyed.

	gwam per line	12"	10"
1 Your break for lunch is short.		30	36
2 The dog barked at the full moon.		32	38
3 The small bird flew into the tree.		34	41
4 The coach called time on the player.		36	43
5 Plan fun things during your free time.		38	46
6 Eating a big lunch will make you sleepy.		40	48
7 The man will get into town this afternoon.		42	50
8 The books are to be returned to the library.		44	53
9 Listen to what is being said by your teachers.		46	55
10 Do not forget to take the makeup test next week.		48	58
11 The phone rang eight times before it was answered.		50	60
12 Do not let the animals in the other room bother you.		52	62

gwam	1'	1	2	3	4	5	6	7	8	9	10
	30"	2	4	6	8	10	12	14	16	18	20

		gwam	1'	2'	3'

SEA TURTLES

Turtle is a common name for an old order of reptiles. The shell, covering the main parts of their body, more or less helps to protect their heads and feet. Just as turtles have long been a source of food for people, their shells have been used for many years in making fine ornaments. Also, their shells are quite strong. A person having the same support could hold up to two large elephants. Turtles are not often seen out of water; some types can stay under the water for days on end. Yet, during birth, they put their eggs on land and then leave the young to care for themselves. Last, they often grow to a large size and live for a number of years. In fact, one is known to have lived for over a century and a half.

gwam	1'	2'	3'
	13	6	4
	27	13	9
	41	20	14
	55	27	18
	69	34	23
	83	42	28
	98	49	33
	112	56	37
	127	64	42
	140	70	47
	145	73	48

PHILATELY

The collection and study of stamps is called philately; it will bring to you many hours of pleasure and will be quite a learning adventure. First, try to start with a small group of stamps in order to learn about the many basic types of stamps that are in use. Later, you will want to buy a large group and learn more than just the basic facts about them. You will begin to learn about the kind of paper which was used, about the countries that made the stamps, and about the different types of design which evolved. Also, you will be able to learn a lot about the process that was used in the printing and how that process changed from year to year. The more active collector soon wants to expand the size of his or her supply.

gwam	1'	2'	3'
	13	7	4
	28	13	9
	42	21	14
	57	28	19
	71	35	24
	85	42	28
	100	49	33
	114	56	40
	128	64	43
	142	71	47
	147	73	49

gwam	1'	1	2	3	4	5	6	7	8	9	10	11	12	13	14
	2'		1		2		3		4		5		6		7	

People have always noted the character of each season and | 4 | 3 | 74

tried to arrange their ~~lives~~ *activities* as well as they could according to | 8 | 5 | 77

changes in the weather.   Most peo_ple like a particular season and what | 13 | 8 | 80

one person may veiw as good weather is often ~~not satisfactory~~ *unsatisfactory* | 17 | 10 | 82

to another.   Some people prefer warm weather, sunny skies, and | 21 | 13 | 85

gentle winds of summer.   Others like the brisk winds *and* snowy | 27 | 15 | 87

weather of winter.   The farmer depends upon all the seasons. | 30 | 18 | 90

The snow and rain of winter and spring ~~is~~ *are* needed to pre_pare | 34 | 20 | 92

ground and nourish the crops; and the warm, sunny weather of | 38 | 23 | 95

summer and fall is needed *to bring the crops to maturity.* | 42 | 25 | 97

The sun has a major effect on the weather.   It gives off a con- | 46 | 28 | 99

siderable a_ount *m* of energy from its surface.   When some of this | 50 | 30 | 102

energy reaches the earth, the surface and air is warmed.   During | 54 | 33 | 105

the summer, the earth's surface is *tilted* toward the sun, receiving a | 59 | 35 | 107

maximum *amount* of energy.   During the winter, the earth is tilted away | 64 | 38 | 110

from the sun, receiving a less amount.   This energy warm_s air, | 68 | 41 | 113

land, and water.   When the water is warmed, it evaporates into | 72 | 43 | 115

the air and becomes clouds.   The clouds cool and become heavy. | 76 | 46 | 118

The water will then fall back to the ~~earth~~ *surface* in the form of rain | 81 | 49 | 120

or other precipita_tion. | 82 | 49 | 121

The total amount of water on earth never changes; it merely | 86 | 52 | 124

changes as it travels from one location to another.   Oceans | 90 | 54 | 126

are the principal source of water entering into the at_mosphere. | 95 | 57 | 129

Consequently, all precipitation has at one time *or another* come from an | 99 | 60 | 132

ocean, even though that particular ocean may be thousands of | 103 | 62 | 134

mile away.   ~~When~~ *As* a droplet of water condenses in the air, it | 107 | 65 | 136

may changes its shape as often as fifty times a second.   When the | 112 | 67 | 139

droplet becomes heavier than the atmosphere whic_h it is in, | 116 | 70 | 141

it will return to earth *to begin its way back to an ocean.* | 120 | 72 | 144

ANTS

		gwam	3'		5'

Although it is thought that people have only been on this earth 4 | 3 | 73
for a few million years, ants have been living here for more than fifty 9 | 5 | 76
million years. The wasp is thought to be one of their early ancestors. 14 | 8 | 79
There are many different species of ants, but they all like a warm cli- 19 | 11 | 82
mate. Over the years, they have changed to meet the needs of life, and 23 | 14 | 85
they have found ways to work and to live with others of their kind. As 28 | 17 | 88
a result, they have set up a social order that is very complex. That 33 | 20 | 90
they have had success can be seen by the fact that they are numerous 37 | 22 | 93
and able to live in various nesting sites and still find food. 42 | 25 | 96

In order to understand how the ant can see, feel, and work in its 46 | 28 | 98
small world, the parts of its body need to be known. The principal parts 51 | 30 | 101
include the head, thorax, and abdomen, and the skeleton is on the out- 55 | 33 | 104
side. They have two eyes, six legs, four jaws that move from side to 60 | 36 | 107
side rather than up and down, and sense-of-touch organs all over the body 65 | 39 | 110
to help them feel their way through the environment. Because much of 70 | 42 | 112
their life is spent in the dark, the senses of touch and smell are far 74 | 45 | 115
more important than those of sight and sound. 77 | 46 | 117

With little doubt, ants can be a problem for people. Because they 82 | 49 | 120
use some of the same materials that people do, they can be a pest. One 87 | 52 | 123
kind of ant can cut off all the leaves of a plant in a single night; 91 | 55 | 125
another kind has a bad sting that can be harmful to animals. They are 96 | 58 | 128
certainly a problem when it comes to human food. Often they will enter a 101 | 61 | 131
house in great numbers looking for food that may have been left out; 106 | 63 | 134
they can ruin a picnic with little effort. It is said that some kinds 110 | 66 | 137
of ants can free a house from insects. Even though this may be true, 115 | 69 | 140
they are more of a headache than an aid. 118 | 71 | 141

gwam 3' | 1 | 2 | 3 | 4 | 5
5' | 1 | 2 | 3

KEYSTROKING DRILL

Key each line twice; repeat if time permits. **Line:** 70 characters **Goal:** Key the rough-draft sentences quickly; concentrate on proofreader's marks.

Rough-Draft Copy

1 you will be asked to ~~complete~~ *fill out* an application form when you seek a job.

2 Before writing a check, *#* Record it *first* in the check register. *or stub*

3 It is important to know how to handle *¶* risk when dealing w ith business.

4 Computers af fect in so many ways our lives while in school or at *lc* HOME.

5 When *you* ~~opening~~ a savings account, you ~~should~~ *must* decide what plan is yours. *for you*

6 ~~Salespeople~~ *Clerks* who earn on ly a commission work ~~work~~ on a commission basis. *straight*

7 conserving our limited time *stet* and natural resources is im perative *today* ~~now~~.

8 To be a *good* shopper, *you* Buy only what you can use at ~~at~~ the ~~right~~ price. *lust*

9 A time card shows the hours and earnings of a ~~WORKER~~. *# is used to worked lc*

10 The total for all your education *is* an investment ~~for~~ *in* your future.

EMOTIONS

	gwam	1'	3'

Many words are used ~~for~~ *to describe* many different *types of* emotions, such as **14 | 5 | 85**

ang er, fear, happ ines, sorrow, and so forth. *An* Emotion, in **26 | 9 | 89**

general, is any mental and physical reaction felt *subjectively* by a person **41 | 14 | 94**

as strong fee ling, causing him or her to prepare for action. **53 | 18 | 98**

An emotion felt by *one* a person is different f rom that felt by **66 | 22 | 102**

any other person in a s imilar instance. *Because* An emotion felt under **80 | 27 | 107**

any circumstance is unique for the person feeling the emotion, **92 | 31 | 111**

the facts of an incident observed by that person will seem **104 | 35 | 115**

different from the *same* facts when they are observed by ~~any~~ *another* person. **118 | 39 | 120**

All emotion have one *characteristic* ~~thing~~ in commmon: The person feeling **13 | 44 | 124**

the emotion is aroused. The action the person performs, *however,* is **27 | 49 | 129**

determined by the type of emotion f elt. If a person feels **39 | 52 | 133**

happy, he *or she* will probably smile, laugh, and ~~be~~ relaxed. If the **52 | 57 | 137**

person feel s angry or afraid, he *or she* will probably be tense, will **66 | 61 | 142**

act hostile towards the pers on or thing that caused the fear **78 | 65 | 146**

or anger, or may cry. Close observation of the action of persons for **92 | 70 | 151**

any period of time can often tell the emotions they are feel- **104 | 74 | 155**

ing during *that* ~~the~~ period. To understand the cause of an emotion **117 | 78 | 159**

is the fi rst step to control it. **123 | 80 | 161**

PYRAMID PARAGRAPHS

Line: 70 characters
Goal: Build speed. Key each line of the paragraph within 15", 12", or 10".

Break through your speed ceiling.
Key: 1' timing on the paragraph. If you finish a line before the time in-terval is

called, continue to the next line; if not, repeat the unfinished line.

	gwam 1'
When a business decides to	5
purchase a computer, much lead	11
time is required from the time the	18
order is placed until the equipment is	26
delivered. When custom programs are to be	34
developed, it may take additional months until	43
they are ready. When the new computer arrives, it	53
may be placed in a special room prepared for it since	64
it is sensitive to heat and dirty air. After the computer	76
is installed, a decision might have to be made about supplies.	88

gwam 1' | 1 | 2 | 3 | 4 | 5 | 6 | 7 | 8 | 9 | 10 | 11 | 12 | 13 |

YOUR PERSONALITY

	gwam 3'	5'
Your personality includes all those traits which set you apart as	4	3 59
an individual. No two people are the same. Each person has good and bad	9	6 62
points. Each person has his or her own way of doing things. Each person	14	9 65
is unique in his or her own way. Your traits are shown by how you look,	19	11 68
what you say, how you feel, and what you do.	22	13 70
How you look is important. Do your clothes fit your personality?	26	16 72
Are they right for your job or the business where you will be working?	31	19 75
How do you wear your clothes? Are they clean and properly fitted? One	36	22 78
of the rules to follow when you apply for a job is to dress the same way	41	25 81
as you would on the job. The right clothes are important, but you must	46	27 84
realize also that good grooming and health are necessary to give a good	51	30 87
impression. It is important that you take a bath daily. Be sure to have	55	33 90
clean hair and teeth. If you do all these things, you will look your	60	36 92
best on the job.	61	37 93
It is quite important to consider how well you listen and what you	66	39 96
say. You should pay attention to what is being said by others. Also,	70	42 99
the words you use to express your thoughts and the tone of your voice	75	45 101
plays a major role in how others perceive you to be. The way you feel	80	48 104
is reflected by the way you act. The way you feel about other people and	85	51 107
the way you treat them are vital. If your personality does not fit a job	90	54 110
position, it is certain that you will be unhappy with the job.	94	56 113

gwam 3' | 1 | 2 | 3 | 4 | 5 |
5' | 1 | 2 | 3 |

**CPA
EXAMINATION**

A certified public accountant offers services to the public for 4 | 3 | 71
a fee. A person who serves as a certified public accountant must hold 9 | 5 | 74
a certificate issued by one of the 50 states. A survey made in late 14 | 8 | 77
1989 showed that the criteria for the certificate vary among the 50 18 | 11 | 79
states. There was an increase in the participation in 1989 from prior 23 | 14 | 82
years. There were 142,135 candidates who took the examination in 1989. 28 | 17 | 85
This exceeds by 452 the 1983 record of 141,683. 31 | 19 | 87

There is some concern with the low number of first-time candidates 35 | 21 | 90
with degrees beyond the baccalaureate. In May 1989, 9.5% of the candi- 40 | 24 | 92
dates had achieved an advanced degree. Nearly 90% of all first-time 45 | 27 | 95
candidates with no advanced degrees were accounting majors. There is 49 | 30 | 98
a high correlation between a person's grade-point average and success 54 | 32 | 101
on the exam. Among the first-time candidates in May 1989 with under- 59 | 35 | 104
graduate grade-point averages of 3.5 to 4.0, 34.5% passed all parts of 63 | 38 | 106
the exam, 18.1% for those with a 3.0 to 3.49 average, 9.4% with a 2.5 68 | 41 | 109
to 2.99 average, and 5.9% with an average of 2.0 to 2.49. The higher 73 | 44 | 112
your grade-point average is the better your quality of performance will 77 | 46 | 115
be on the exam subjects. 79 | 47 | 116

The candidates seem to take the exam earlier in their careers and 83 | 50 | 119
to have less work experience. Candidates with one or more years of 88 | 53 | 121
public accounting experience showed a 21.6% passing rate, followed by 93 | 56 | 124
those in business (20.6%), and then in government with 18.2%. Based 97 | 58 | 127
on the 1989 study, the certified public accountant exam is hard. Only 102 | 61 | 130
about 20% of the candidates passed all subjects the first time they 107 | 64 | 132
took them. It is realized that there will be a great need for certified 111 | 67 | 135
public accountants in the years to come. 114 | 68 | 137

gwam 3' | 1 | 2 | 3 | 4 | 5 |
     5' | 1 | 2 | 3 |

LISTENING

It has been said that because we have two ears and one mouth we | 4 | 3 | 73

should listen more than we talk. Most of what we know is a result of | 9 | 5 | 76

listening. It may be described as what we hear, what we understand, | 13 | 8 | 78

and what we remember. Because of listening, we know how to talk and to | 18 | 11 | 81

read; we learn most job skills in this way. All people in the busi- | 23 | 14 | 84

ness world must listen—to a supervisor, to an employee, to a customer, | 28 | 17 | 87

and to other workers. Yet a problem common to all of us is the lack of | 32 | 19 | 90

ability to listen and to receive instructions in a clear and correct | 37 | 22 | 93

manner. The fact is, we remember less than a fourth of what we hear. | 42 | 25 | 95

If we make an effort, all of us can improve our listening skills. | 46 | 28 | 98

To do this, we must learn to listen with an open mind so that we will | 51 | 30 | 101

hear what is actually said. An open mind is alert and ready to receive | 55 | 33 | 104

facts without making a decision until the speaker is through. We must | 60 | 36 | 106

not let prejudices interfere with what is being said. It is hard to be | 65 | 39 | 109

objective about ideas that we have held for a long time. We must not | 70 | 42 | 112

assume that we have all the facts only to find out later that we do not. | 74 | 45 | 115

We must be careful not to reject ideas which are new or which contradict | 79 | 48 | 118

that which we now believe. | 81 | 49 | 119

When people speak, they do not speak in a way that is so well organ- | 86 | 51 | 122

ized that important ideas are obvious. Thus, we need to learn to evalu- | 90 | 54 | 125

ate that which we hear. In order to do this, we need to have goals and | 95 | 57 | 127

be alert to them so that the main ideas can be selected from what is | 100 | 60 | 130

being said. If we do not hear these main ideas, then we need to ask | 104 | 63 | 133

questions. There is a lot more to the art of listening than just hearing | 109 | 66 | 136

and blocking out what is not needed. Try and improve your listening | 114 | 68 | 139

skills by following some of the ideas given above. | 117 | 70 | 141

gwam 3' | 1 | 2 | 3 | 4 | 5
5' | 1 | 2 | 3

KEYSTROKING DRILL

Key each line twice; repeat if time permits.

Line: 70 characters
Goal: Keep your eyes on the copy; relax and make each reach without moving the hand forward.

Numbers and Symbols

The owner ordered 146 chairs, 30 tables, 28 lamps, and 573 trash cans.
Forty-two doctors, 190 lawyers, 2,351 teachers, 8,467 nurses attended.
Their inventory listed seven 100-gallon drums and 11 five-gallon cans.
This 1991 rule is discussed in Volume 5, pages 367, 842, 945 and 1022.
Ben grew from 4' 10" in 1990 to 5' 8" in 1992; he gained 25 lbs. also.
Their rates jumped from 7 1/2% to 8 1/4% and back to 6 3/4% last year.
They moved from 2135-A Carol Drive to 4089 North 67th Street in Salem.
Flight #290 left at 8:45 on 4/9/91 with 257 people (44 were children).
Costs of Items A, B, and C are $203.51, $.67, and $4.89, respectively.
The two meetings of PBL were held at 4:30 p.m. and 9:30 p.m. on 3/4/91.
Lost certificates ABC610-3-54 and CPR278-5-43 will cost him $9,722.57.

---

gwam 1' | 3'

HIGHWAY FUNDING

In the last fiscal year, the state expenditure for capital outlay | 13 | 4 | 91
ranked 46th in the nation. The budget for state highways is suffering | 27 | 9 | 96
from a huge deficit. Our $.12 per gallon tax is beneath all but 5 other | 42 | 14 | 101
states. The current tax schedule, which was initiated in 1971, has | 56 | 19 | 105
not undergone a significant change for a longer period of time than | 69 | 23 | 110
the rates of all but 6 other states. House Bill 564 will create a $.06 | 84 | 28 | 115
increase in the gasoline tax and an increase of 17% in various trans- | 97 | 32 | 119
portation fees. The citizens will vote on this bill on 11/04. During | 112 | 37 | 124
the next 2 years, only $7,022,386.45 has been appropriated for the | 125 | 42 | 129
completion of State Highway 74-76 to the junction of Interstate 40. | 138 | 46 | 133
These monies are inadequate. | 144 | 48 | 135

A gasoline tax increase of $.05 per gallon is mandatory if we are | 13 | 52 | 139
to reduce the huge highway deficit. Yet, the voters have rejected $.04 | 28 | 57 | 144
and $.05 increases in the past. It is doubtful that they will accept | 42 | 62 | 149
a $.05 tax. Hence, the state has lost $157,388,901 in transportation | 56 | 66 | 153
revenues. The citizens are requesting a 26% cut in property tax. As | 70 | 71 | 158
highway construction is only one of many costly ventures now under | 84 | 76 | 163
consideration, a new form of local support is needed to assist the state | 98 | 80 | 167
in meeting increased costs. New revenues may be derived by creative | 111 | 85 | 172
financing on the local level. | 117 | 87 | 174

gwam 1' | 1 | 2 | 3 | 4 | 5 | 6 | 7 | 8 | 9 | 10 | 11 | 12 | 13 | 14 |
3' | 1 | 2 | 3 | 4 | 5 |

KEYSTROKING DRILL

Key the entire drill one time; repeat if time permits. Use the tabulator key.   *Line:* 76 characters; set tabs every 17 spaces.   *Goal:* Tab quickly after each set of phrases; return without looking up.

to do	to do so	if it	if it is
to go	to go to	he is	he is to
and the	and to do the	and go	and go to the
to show	to show them	they may	they may go
agree with you	our letter	no longer than	if you must
get my tax	window pane	best song	running water
cast in iron	quiet moment	shoe shine	beautiful cake
few minutes	say nothing but	turn the light	large envelope
in a moment	is it sound	please try to	close the piano
federal tax	world peace	stand tall	short haircut
clean clothes	nice looking	a thick book	luxury car
social systems	good night	picture frame	new skateboard

	gwam	1'	2'	3'
SAVING ANTIQUES	Saving antiques goes back as far in time as when gems were kept in	13	7	4
	temples for ages. Today, the supply of antiques is limited as more	27	13	9
	people are now interested in the old things they own and are hanging on	41	21	14
	to them. They know more about these items than they did a few years	55	27	18
	ago. There is no set age that an item must be to be called an antique,	70	35	23
	but most dealers do agree that an item should be at least a hundred	83	41	28
	years old. Some people think that age is the only thing which goes into	97	49	33
	making an item an antique. Such things as aesthetic, historic, and finan-	110	56	37
	cial value are vital too.	117	59	39
	Naming an antique piece frequently takes a lot of research. If it	13	65	44
	is possible, contact an expert who knows his or her items very well;	27	72	48
	this person may be able to name it for you. If not, visit a local art	41	79	53
	gallery or museum, as you may find the answer there. Check in all types	56	86	58
	of books to help you in your search. If the item is not listed in a	70	93	62
	book, your task is more difficult. Visit the antique stores in your	83	100	67
	town to see if a similar item can be found. If you cannot carry the	97	107	72
	item with you, take a picture of it. Do not depend too much on what	111	114	76
	family members may tell you because their memories may fail them.	124	121	81

gwam	1'	1	2	3	4	5	6	7	8	9	10	11	12	13	14
	2'		1		2		3		4		5		6		7

LIMITATIONS OF OUR EARTH

	gwam	3'	5'

Before the first explorers went into outer space, many persons thought of the world as large and endless. Humans have explored the world for many centuries, and throughout most of that time, the earth continued to provide new land and resources for people to discover.

Yet, the advent of space travel has forced us to recognize that our world is limited in size and that the space and resources available here are very valuable to us.

Because the earth's population continues to increase quickly, problems concerned with lack of space are becoming more and more serious. Much of the earth's surface is covered by water, leaving about seven billion acres of land for human use. This may sound like a large amount of space, but it has been estimated that in twenty years only about one acre of useful space will be available per person. This one acre apiece will have to provide us with food, support our homes, and house our industries.

Our problems with energy have become just as significant as our problems with space. The quality of our lives is greatly dependent on energy, and in our efforts to maintain our current standard of living, we are depleting the earth's mineral resources at an alarming rate. But there are several sources of energy that we have not yet learned to accommodate to our needs. If we wish to continue to live well on this planet, we will have to find ways to develop these new energy sources.

gwam column values (3', then additional column, then 5'):
3 | 2 | 59
7 | 4 | 61
11 | 6 | 63
15 | 9 | 66
18 | 11 | 68
21 | 13 | 70
25 | 15 | 72
29 | 17 | 74
29 | 17 | 74
33 | 20 | 76
36 | 22 | 79
40 | 24 | 81
44 | 26 | 83
48 | 29 | 85
51 | 31 | 88
56 | 33 | 90
59 | 36 | 92
62 | 37 | 94
66 | 39 | 96
69 | 42 | 98
73 | 44 | 101
77 | 46 | 103
81 | 49 | 105
85 | 51 | 108
88 | 53 | 110
92 | 55 | 112
95 | 57 | 114

NAUTICAL TERMS

It is impossible to live near a body of water and not become inter-   4 | 3 | 86

ested in boats. Once you do, you may want to purchase your own. This   9 | 5 | 90

will take a lot of thought. There are so many types, and each has its   14 | 8 | 92

own particular use. For the purpose of learning some of the parts of a   19 | 11 | 95

boat, I will discuss a cabin cruiser, which is designed for pleasure.   23 | 14 | 98

To begin with, everything on or about a boat has a proper name. The   28 | 17 | 101

covered part where people can live is the cabin. It is designed for   33 | 20 | 104

comfort. If you stand in the back in the partly covered cockpit and   37 | 22 | 106

face forward, you will be looking at the pointed end, which is the bow.   42 | 25 | 109

Behind you at the very back is the flat end, which is called the stern.   47 | 28 | 112

As you stand looking forward, the side of the boat on your right   51 | 31 | 115

is the starboard side. The port side is on your left. Depending upon   56 | 33 | 118

the design, size, and weight of the boat, some of it will extend below   61 | 36 | 120

the water line. The floor is called a deck; that part covering the bow   65 | 39 | 123

is called the foredeck. A hatch is an open section of the deck which is   70 | 42 | 126

used to go below. Below is a term you will often use; it means to go   75 | 45 | 129

below the deck. When moving through the water, you are under way. In   80 | 48 | 132

order to know where you are going and the manner in which you will get   84 | 51 | 135

there, you will need to read a chart. If you want to become knowledge-   89 | 53 | 137

able about boats, you will need to review these terms several times.   94 | 56 | 140

Are you ready to learn a few more terms? To make fast is used when   98 | 59 | 143

you want to keep the boat from moving. On each side of the cockpit are   103 | 62 | 146

open points called scuppers, which permit water to run off. An anchor   107 | 65 | 149

is attached by a line and placed in the water when you want to hold the   112 | 67 | 151

boat in a particular place. The end of the boat where the anchor is   117 | 70 | 154

attached is called the outboard end, while the other end is called the   122 | 73 | 157

inboard end. The outside of the boat is the topsides, and its height   126 | 76 | 160

is called the freeboard. The more weight carried on board, the less   131 | 79 | 163

is the freeboard because the boat is lower in the water. Keep trying   136 | 81 | 165

to learn these terms, as well as new ones, in the months to come.   140 | 84 | 168

gwam 3'	1	2	3	4	5
5'	1		2		3

PYRAMID PARAGRAPHS

Line: 70 characters
Goal: Build speed. Key each line of the paragraph within 15", 12", or 10".

Strive to key each line within the time limit. Repeat the goal for the second paragraph.

Key: 1' timing on each paragraph. If you finish a line before the time interval is called, continue to the next line; if not, repeat the unfinished line.

	gwam 1'
Business managers must have effective leader-	9
ship skills. Managers influence others toward the	19
accomplishment of aims and objectives. Influence comes	30
to leaders from formal or informal settings. Formal leaders	42
are usually appointed by the business. They use the positions to	56
bring to pass the goals of the business. They utilize every resource.	70

	gwam 1'
Informal leaders normally tend to emerge from	9
within groups. These informal leaders do have the	19
charismatic power to guide and direct the other members	30
within their group. A formal leader may have all the rights	42
of leadership; however, these rights will not necessarily inspire	56
others to attain goals. Informal leaders can accomplish goals easier.	70

gwam 1' | 1 | 2 | 3 | 4 | 5 | 6 | 7 | 8 | 9 | 10 | 11 | 12 | 13 | 14 |

SOCIAL SECURITY SYSTEM

	gwam 1'	3'
Social security is a governmental insurance program to pro-	12	4 71
vide income for workers who are retired or disabled. Numerous	24	8 75
workers in the United States are part of the social security system.	38	13 80
During the many years of working, they contribute into a special	51	17 84
trust fund. Each employer pays a matching amount. When a	63	21 88
worker's earnings are either stopped or reduced because of	75	25 92
illness, injury, or retirement; the worker begins to receive	87	29 96
a monthly check. The check's amount that will be paid	98	33 100
each month on retirement is determined by the earnings of a	110	37 104
worker for his or her entire career. An average of the earnings	123	41 108
is used to calculate the amount of the monthly check. So-	135	45 112
cial security is a program that affects just about all of us,	147	49 116
including those who are self-employed, disabled or surviv-	159	53 120
ing members of the insured worker. If you do not yet have	170	57 124
a social security card, you would be wise to apply for	181	60 128
one. The number of your card is used to maintain a record	193	64 132
of your earnings after you commence working.	202	67 135

KEYSTROKING DRILL

Key the drill once as shown; if time permits, rekey.

Line: 70 characters.
Goal: Move the fourth finger to the shift key smoothly, hold firmly, and release quickly.

Shift Key and Caps Lock Key

Utah Oregon Maine Idaho Hawaii Nebraska Illinois Pennsylvania Maryland Juneau Phoenix Hartford Olympia Providence Nashville Montpelier Pierre James Madison James K. Polk Lyndon Johnson Herbert Hoover John Kennedy

Alaska Virginia Colorado Texas Wyoming South Dakota Tennessee Delaware Denver Cheyenne Trenton Baton Rouge Raleigh Austin Charleston Bismarck Ronald Reagan Gerald Ford Calvin Coolidge Chester Arthur Zachary Taylor

OSHA | AMTRAK | IBM Corp. | AT&T Co. | NCR Corp. | H&R Block, Inc. | The GAP, Inc. THE PHANTOM OF THE OPERA by A. L. Webber | DRIVING MISS DAISY by A. Uhry The U.S. GNP NOW Accounts | the availability of ATM's | FOB shipping point

LIMITED RESOURCES

	gwam	3'	5'
It is a fact that economic resources are used to produce goods and	4	3	83
services. It can be said that the amount of resources that we have to	9	5	86
use decides the amount of goods and services to be produced. There is a	14	8	88
limited quantity of the resources found in an economic system at any	19	11	91
given time. A firm may produce a wide range of goods. There seems to be	24	14	94
a wide range of services that are to be used with the factors of produc-	28	17	97
tion. Thus, goods and services are in short supply for most of our use.	33	20	100
Therefore, a system will not be in a position to meet all the wants and	38	23	103
needs of its people. A want is something you desire but could live	43	26	106
without, such as a car. A need is something you must have if you are to	47	28	109
survive, such as food. It may be hard to decide whether something is a	52	31	111
need or a want. We will have to cope with these wants and needs in the	57	34	114
years to come.	58	35	115
One of the primary purposes of an economic system is to turn the	62	37	117
factors of production into goods and services. There are so many things	67	40	120
people want. In fact, it seems that the more people have, the more	72	43	123
they want. Most people want to have more than the basic needs of life.	77	46	126
Most would like to have a few luxuries, too. When a want is fulfilled,	81	49	129
another one can quickly take its place. It would not be far from the	86	52	132
truth to say that there is no end to our wants and desires.	90	54	134
One must realize that the amount of goods and services that can be	94	57	137
produced at any point in time is limited. Yet, most people now seem to	99	60	140
have more and more wants. It is just not possible in an economic system	104	62	143
to satisfy all the wants of all the people. When there are more goods	109	65	145
and services desired than what are produced, those items are said to be	114	68	148
in short supply. This is a problem faced by each economic system. One	118	71	151
way of dealing with those items is to limit the use of a good or ser-	123	74	154
vice. A possible way to deal with a shortage might be to use some other	128	77	157
good or service, or it might be best to sell them to those who want them	132	80	160
the most.	133	80	160

gwam 3' | 1 | 2 | 3 | 4 | 5 |
5' | 1 | 2 | 3 |

ESTABLISHING CREDIT

	gwam 3'	5'
Throughout your life you are establishing your credit rating. This	4 · 3	76
credit rating is a measure used to determine if you are going to be a	9 · 5	79
good credit risk. Two factors that determine a credit rating are the	14 · 8	82
person's record for paying bills on time and holding a steady job. To	19 · 11	85
realize that you have an excellent credit rating enables you to borrow	23 · 14	87
money easily or to purchase on credit. A good credit rating is some-	28 · 17	90
thing you should earn.	29 · 18	91
An integral part of your credit rating is your behavior, personal	34 · 20	94
qualities, and how you conduct yourself. Are you dependable in school?	39 · 23	97
On the job? When paying your bills? When speaking of credit, it is	43 · 26	99
essential to repay what has been loaned to you. With earning power,	48 · 29	102
you must pay back what you buy on credit. As you expect to be known	52 · 31	105
as an excellent credit risk, what assets have you acquired? If you	57 · 34	108
have an automobile, you are a better risk than a person without such an	62 · 37	110
asset. A savings account affects positively your credit rating. Your	66 · 40	113
credit rating is on file with a credit bureau. A lender can go to the	71 · 43	116
bureau and request data on you. A report, called a credit history,	76 · 45	119
will be sent to the lender. This report contains information on your	80 · 48	122
previous credit experiences and your paying track record.	84 · 50	124
You must have something on record to establish a credit history.	89 · 53	127
To initially get credit, you may decide to open a savings or checking	93 · 56	129
account. If you save regularly, this indicates you are capable of	98 · 59	132
managing money and keeping records. Another option is to apply for a	102 · 61	135
charge account at a store. Your charge account will be proof of your	107 · 64	138
financial stability. Many firms use a scoring system to decide if you	112 · 67	141
should get credit. The point total measures a person's credit rating.	117 · 70	143
You will realize that credit should be used wisely. You want to be a	121 · 73	146
good credit risk.	122 · 73	147

gwam 3' | 1 | 2 | 3 | 4 | 5
5' | 1 | 2 | 3

APPLICATION LETTER

Do you know how to write a letter of application? You will want to write this type of letter when the job you are seeking is in another city, when you are answering an ad, or when you mail a cover letter with your resume. The application letter is one way to get a job interview. There are two types of letters. One type is when you do not know a job exists. Your letter should show your interest in working for the firm, should list your skills and traits, and should ask about a job opening. The second type of letter is used in response to some news that a job exists. You will want to write both types to locate a job.

When you write a letter of application, you must realize that it is a sales letter. You are the product. The letter will show the skills you have to offer and try to convince the employer to consider you for the job. The employer can compare your skills and traits with the requirements of the job. You must plan your letter so that it will get results. You may want to include a resume. If you do, you need to refer to it in the letter. It is important to list all your skills that may help you to get the job. Close the letter by asking for an interview. An interview will give you a chance to discuss your traits and skills for the job with the employer.

It is paramount to make a good impression with your letter. Key your letter on good paper that is a standard size. Use white paper only. Your return address is to be keyed above the date. In some cases, your letter may separate from the resume. Thus, you should put your mailing address on both the letter and the resume. Did you address the letter to a person? You should try to check the name of the person so that you can use the exact name. You may have to call the firm to verify the name. Try to confine the letter to one page. Since you have detailed all the facts in the resume, you may just need two or three paragraphs in the letter. Any letter style can be used, but be sure the letter is neat and centered on the page.

	3'	5'
	4	3	84
	9	5	87
	14	8	90
	19	11	93
	24	14	96
	28	17	99
	33	20	101
	38	23	104
	42	25	107
	46	28	109
	51	31	112
	56	34	115
	61	36	118
	65	39	121
	70	42	124
	75	45	127
	80	48	129
	84	51	132
	86	52	133
	91	54	136
	96	57	139
	101	60	142
	105	63	145
	110	66	148
	115	69	151
	120	72	153
	124	75	156
	129	78	159
	134	81	162
	136	82	163

gwam 3' | 1 | 2 | 3 | 4 | 5 |
5' | 1 | 2 | 3 |

KEYSTROKING DRILL

Key each line twice; repeat if time permits.

Line: 70 characters

Goal: Key each group of response patterns with continuity.

Letter Response

be put tax out red day vet ink saw fur joy say cut bad ply their queue
some rush wash cute buoy wish blue wild kill down jump papa lump eerie
to the that was when will it shall go to why was can do set up the tab

Word Response

it shall | shall be | it shall be | it has | has not | it has not | it is not time
will be | be in | in time | will be in time | now is the time | the time is gone
was not | not able | was not able | but not | not now | but not now | not able now

Combination Response

in the world | it did happen | it will end | cannot go now | will talk to your
did you know | drop me a line | let me know | call me later | shall let you go
as soon as | if it is convenient | do not reply | cope with it | please excuse

---

	gwam	1'	3'

SOLE PRO-PRIETORSHIP

You will eventually be entering the business environment. You may	13	4	93
be working for yourself or others. The most prevalent type of owner-	27	9	98
ship is the sole proprietorship. It is so easy to start. A person who	42	14	103
wants to operate a business and has the finances to do so may start a	56	18	108
sole proprietorship. A person starting a business must comply with the	70	23	112
governmental regulations that are applicable to business in general and	84	28	117
to that person's business in particular. It often includes registering	99	33	122
as a collector of state and local sales taxes. The official name of the	113	38	127
business, in addition to other pertinent data about the owner, needs to	128	43	132
be filed in a public office. This is required by law so that the public	142	47	136
will know with whom they may be dealing.	150	50	139

The owner is responsible for managing the business. The profits	13	54	143
made from the business belong to the owner, but so do the losses. This	27	59	148
type of business is flexible; it permits the owner to manage as he or	41	64	153
she wishes. No special legal procedure is needed to establish this	55	68	157
form of business, but the owner should get sound advice from a recog-	69	73	162
nized accountant. If a small business does not have enough capital to	83	78	167
continue to operate, it may just go out of business. Unless the owner	97	82	172
gives the business to another person, the business ceases to exist when	112	87	176
the owner dies or retires.	117	89	178

gwam	1'	1	2	3	4	5	6	7	8	9	10	11	12	13	14
	3'		1			2			3			4			5	

PART 2

AVERAGE COPY

Part 2 continues to emphasize speed-building and technique drills with reinforcement on keystroking patterns, response patterns, and machine parts.

Goals for each drill are included to improve keystroking power.

Part 2 includes 1', 3', and 5' triple-controlled timed writings of average difficulty (syllable intensity, 1.53; average word length, 5.7; high-frequency words, 80%). Copy in script and rough draft is also presented.

KEYSTROKING DRILL

Key the entire drill once; repeat if time permits.

Line: 70 characters

Goal: Read with care as you key; wrists up; elbows in.

	Key	
Specific Keys	p	cup par pat part top stop post past pass step pep pop plump pip up pan
	x	tax fix six mix nix relax flax sax vex fox lax wax text flex fax xylem
	n	no not in nine and hand won now own none now known ton son moon end
	q	quick quiet quaint query quote quell quest squad quart quasi quip quiz
	c	cut count court account cede cuff cot cat cute cite cope cold cave can
	w	we were well law was wash wish with ware wore watt when worn crew sewn
	g	go got fig golf flag judge right eight gone glow gain gape gap gum rag
	d	did read lead good need deed dance dare edit said does doe raid dot do
	z	zone zig zilch fizz zag zombie size prize zip zoo zap dozen maze maize
	b	buy boy but box big be bet best beat bib black back buoy bomb born bay
	m	man men most more mine mind might mite made maid milk mop mat mow
	r	crew serve try report rezone river radio expert fore or rate extra rye
	s	saw is assess see sale said was lost sad sell lost his she sin sad sum
	j	just judge joust join jerk jump joy jury junk jam jell joke jog rejoin

---

PIPES

	gwam	1'	3'
It is not surprising that our language, in itself, is difficult to		13	4 48
learn. Confronted with standard, slang, and regional terms together,		27	9 53
many students will face an unbelievable number of meanings for just a		41	14 58
very simple term. For example, the four-letter word pipe may be some-		55	18 62
thing to be smoked, a simple course, a cheep or chirping sound, vocal		69	23 67
cords or the larynx, or an unrealistic dream. It could also refer to a		84	28 72
deposit zone of ore, an order to be quiet, a trim, or an order in the		98	33 76
navy. The meanings that are listed above have limited association with		112	37 81
what is perhaps the most common use of the word, a cylinder which can		126	42 86
carry liquid, gas, or wires.		132	44 88

gwam	1'	1	2	3	4	5	6	7	8	9	10	11	12	13	14
	3'		1			2			3			4			5	

BUSINESS PLANNING

In the process of developing a business, it is extremely important | 4 | 3 | 69

to plan and organize your activities. Good planning will bring about | 9 | 5 | 72

success. In our daily lives, planning helps us to organize our actions | 14 | 8 | 75

and helps us to achieve our goals. Planning is one of the functions | 18 | 11 | 77

of management. Many owners have skills in one, if not in all, of the | 23 | 14 | 80

functional areas. It is hard to develop the skills needed to satisfy | 28 | 17 | 83

each and every area. It is a known fact that without good planning | 32 | 19 | 86

business firms will fail. Owners realize that they do not know every- | 37 | 22 | 88

thing. They must depend on their personnel, plan their actions, and | 42 | 25 | 91

organize their resources. If all of this is done, then a business has | 46 | 28 | 94

a chance to succeed. It is definitely true that only the well-managed | 51 | 31 | 97

firm, one that has carefully planned its activities, will succeed in | 56 | 33 | 100

the marketplace today. | 57 | 34 | 101

As a business becomes more complex, its activities have to be more | 62 | 37 | 103

carefully planned. How is planning defined? It is the process of de- | 66 | 40 | 106

termining what should be attempted to achieve the objectives of the | 71 | 42 | 109

firm. Planning is a very relevant objective of management. Planning | 75 | 45 | 112

takes place to achieve the company's goals. It involves budgeting and | 80 | 48 | 114

requires much time. It is hard for a small business owner to spend a | 85 | 51 | 117

great amount of time in the planning process. The small business owner | 90 | 54 | 120

often spends much time in solving and handling the problems that are | 94 | 57 | 123

confronting him or her on a daily basis. A small business owner can't | 99 | 59 | 126

afford to take or spend so much time in planning or organizing the activ- | 104 | 62 | 129

ities of the business. Yet a business owner must plan in order to ensure | 109 | 65 | 132

the success of the firm. | 110 | 66 | 133

gwam 3'   1   2   3   4   5

      5'   1   2   3

JOINING AN ORGANIZATION

Do you belong to an organization or uphold a cause? Chances are good that you will be a member of one or more organizations of some type at some time in your life. In our complex society, we as individuals are becoming more and more attracted to organizations. Almost any cause you can think of has an organization, often with a host of affiliates, advocating its ends. In fact, some causes have groups that operate on a nationwide scale and have recognized charters. If you don't belong to an organization now, you probably will in the future.

Whatever your profession, hobby, or opinions may be, there is probably some group or organization with kindred feelings which would like to have you as a member. Thus, as is the case in any of our democratic institutions, participation and hard work are requisites for the success of the group. You may be asked to work on committees, to make periodic reports at membership meetings, or even to assume the leadership of the group. Regardless of the job you choose in the group, be a devoted, working member.

gwam	3'	5'
	4	3 45
	9	5 48
	14	8 51
	19	11 54
	23	14 56
	28	17 59
	33	20 62
	37	22 64
	41	25 67
	46	27 70
	51	30 73
	55	33 76
	60	36 79
	65	39 81
	70	42 84
	71	42 85

INTEREST AND INTEREST RATES

Interest is the fee paid for the use of credit or money. Measured in monetary terms, interest is the difference between the total that is repaid and the sum originally advanced, which is termed the principal. The rate of interest is the ratio between the interest earned during a period of time and the principal originally borrowed. When computing interest, this rate is expressed as a decimal. The traditional unit of time in finance is one year, but other periods of time, such as a month or a day, are sometimes used.

Interest may be computed by one of three processes. If the interest is to be fully paid at the onset of the contract, the charge is termed discount interest. If the interest is to be fully paid at the closing of the contract, it is termed simple interest. If the interest is to be paid in allotments at present times as the contract advances, it becomes compound interest. This type involves interest paid on interest, because the interest that is accrued periodically is added to the existing principal to derive a new principal. The enlarged principal earns more money in the subsequent periods, though the rate stays the same.

gwam	3'	5'
	4	3 49
	9	6 52
	14	8 54
	19	11 57
	23	14 60
	28	17 63
	33	20 66
	35	21 67
	40	24 70
	44	27 73
	49	29 75
	54	32 78
	59	35 81
	64	38 84
	68	41 87
	73	44 90
	77	46 92

gwam 3' |___|___1___|___2___|___3___|___4___|___5___|
     5' |_____1_____|_____2_____|_____3_____|

PYRAMID PARAGRAPHS

Line: 70 characters
Goal: Build speed. Key each line of the paragraph within 15", 12", or 10".

Strive to key each line within the time limit. Repeat the goal for the second paragraph.

Key: 1' timing on each paragraph. If you finish a line before the time interval is called, continue to the next line; if not, repeat the unfinished line.

	gwam 1'
As the wonderful world of roses unfolds, there are	10
many different ways to enjoy them. Their vibrant color	21
is appreciated in the garden. However, roses may be used to	33
produce dusting power, rose beads, and rose water. The petals of	46
roses are used in cooking. Roses are often used as fresh-cut flowers.	60

	gwam 1'
To get enjoyment from your fresh-cut roses, select	10
blossoms that are just opening. Cut roses in the early	21
morning when the plant's moisture is highest. Your cuttings	33
should be placed in a bucket of lukewarm water. Use a clean vase	46
with warm water to arrange the roses. Keep the roses in a cool place.	60

gwam 1' | 1 | 2 | 3 | 4 | 5 | 6 | 7 | 8 | 9 | 10 | 11 | 12 | 13 | 14 |

COMPUTER BENEFITS

	gwam 1'	3'
There are numerous benefits of computers to society. Computers can	14	4 99
be very useful to humans in so many ways. The benefits may be great,	28	9 103
but they do cost a great deal of money. One of the primary benefits of	42	14 108
computers is that they produce valid information. Also, they store and	56	19 113
process much data. Computers are able to create information, which is	71	23 118
the key to good decision making. When you make a decision, you select	85	28 123
one of many options. You are not sure what exactly can happen with each	99	33 127
option. Valid information will help reduce the uncertainty and will	113	38 132
help you to be more positive about the outcomes from your decisions.	127	42 136
With computers, you have improved service. Computers are capable of	14	47 141
operating at any time of the day or night. They can process data faster	28	52 146
than humans. As a result, a business is able to serve its clients more	43	56 151
easily and efficiently. Because of computers, you can recognize better	57	61 156
service in your bank, grocery store, or shoe store. You may be attracted	72	66 161
to a business precisely as a result of this service.	82	70 164
The final benefit of computers is increased productivity. Just	13	74 168
recall how well you can perform in a given period of time with the use of	28	79 173
a computer. If you are quite productive from using a computer, it may	42	84 178
mean that you reduce the costs for a business to produce its goods and	56	88 183
services. Consequently, these savings may be distributed to its clients	71	93 188
in lower prices.	74	94 189

gwam 1' | 1 | 2 | 3 | 4 | 5 | 6 | 7 | 8 | 9 | 10 | 11 | 12 | 13 | 14 |
3' | 1 | 2 | 3 | 4 | 5 |

GUIDED WRITING SENTENCES

Line: 70 characters
Goal: Build speed. Key each sentence in 12" or 10".

Key: 30" or 1' timings on the sentences. If you finish a sentence before the time interval is called, go to the next sentence. For each new timing, continue from last complete sentence keyed.

		gwam per line	12"	10"
1	He failed to concentrate.		25	30
2	Keep your eyes on this object.		30	36
3	The key is where it all originates.		35	42
4	The biggest freeze will come in a month.		40	48
5	The audit was due by the middle of the month.		45	54
6	Any ball game without hot dogs is not a ball game.		50	60
7	A good defensive player always knows where the ball is.		55	66
8	A standing ovation may merely mean that a stretch is needed.		60	72
9	His sense of direction told me that he was not a famous explorer.		65	78
10	He appears to have several of the rings missing in his shower curtain.		70	84

gwam	1'	1	2	3	4	5	6	7	8	9	10	11	12	13	14
	30"	2	4	6	8	10	12	14	16	18	20	22	24	26	28

---

		gwam	1'	3'

SAILING

	gwam 1'	3'
People who sail are usually only too happy to share many exhilarat-	13	4 46
ing tales of this sport. Differences in size and level of complexity	27	9 51
among sailboats are great. They range from the very simple to the highly	42	14 55
computerized. To a knowledgeable sailor, the speed and direction of the	57	19 60
wind are generally not as important as the shape and size of the sails	71	24 65
and keel. These work together to permit the sailor to go in almost any	85	28 70
direction. These beautiful boats can be seen in harbors and bays every	100	33 75
year as more and more people realize how relaxing it is to leave their	114	38 79
schedules behind and meet the challenge of the sea.	124	41 83

DEFENSIVE DRIVING

	gwam 1'	3'
The driver of an automobile is responsible not only for the life of	14	5 46
each person riding in that car, but also for the safety of other drivers	28	9 50
and their passengers. The best protection against accidents is defensive	43	14 55
driving. A defensive driver never takes chances. He or she is aware at	58	19 60
all times of bad road conditions and of the position and speed of each	72	24 65
approaching car. This type of driver avoids getting involved in diffi-	86	29 70
cult situations by trying to be prepared for anything that other drivers	101	34 75
might do. Finally, a defensive driver never insists on taking the right-	115	38 79
of-way at the expense of safety.	122	41 82

gwam	1'	1	2	3	4	5	6	7	8	9	10	11	12	13	14
	3'		1		2		3		4		5				

CONTRACTS

A contract is a legal agreement between two or more competent persons. Each person has certain rights and assumes certain obligations that can be enforced in a court of law. Some contracts are quite easy to understand; for example, buying a book or ordering a pizza. Other contracts, such as buying a car or house, are more complicated. For these contracts, you are asked to sign your name to a formal document. A contract is an agreement that creates a legal obligation that will be enforced by a court. On the other hand, social agreements are not enforceable in the court. The persons do not plan to create a legal obligation.

3'	5'
4	3	81
9	5	84
14	8	87
18	11	89
23	14	92
28	17	95
32	19	98
37	22	101
42	25	103
42	25	104

To create a valid contract, all four elements must be present. They are offer and acceptance, consideration, competent parties, and legal purpose. The first step in forming a contract is an offer. The party making the offer is the offeror. The person to whom the offer is made is the offeree. The offeree must accept an offer. Something of value must be given by each party to bind the agreement, such as property or money. This is consideration. Only competent parties have the legal and mental ability to enter into binding contracts. In the eyes of the law, some parties are not free to enter into contracts. Minors, persons under the influence of drugs or alcohol, and insane persons are examples of persons who are not free to enter into a contract. The purpose of the contract must not be against the law. An illegal agreement is not enforceable in the courts.

3'	5'
47	28	106
51	31	109
56	34	112
61	36	115
65	39	118
70	42	120
75	45	123
80	48	126
84	51	129
89	54	132
94	56	135
100	59	138
101	61	139

If all four elements are present, a contract has been formed. You must remember that if any one element is missing a contract does not exist, and the agreement is not enforceable against either person. When a person does not perform his or her obligation in a contract, the contract has been broken or breached. A person has certain legal remedies to obtain satisfaction, in court if necessary, for an injury caused by breach of contract.

3'	5'
106	63	142
110	66	144
115	69	147
120	72	150
125	75	153
129	78	156
131	78	157

gwam 3' | 1 | 2 | 3 | 4 | 5 |
5' | 1 | 2 | 3 |

CAREER PATHS

In the past, the recognition received by office support staff in regard to position and salary was often tied to the level of advancement of their boss. If the boss received a higher position in management, it was common to see the secretary promoted as well. If the boss was not promoted, often the secretary, even if qualified, also was not promoted. If there is not a direct link between job qualifications and career path, workers become very unhappy with their work.

A firm that has an open career path for its workers offers people a chance to work their way up to management level jobs. When looking for a job, check for these factors in order to know if a firm has open career paths: Is there a description of each job, giving its duties and responsibilities, as well as the qualifications for the job? Does the staff receive good supervision? Are there at least several levels of advancement within each special area? Managerial jobs should be directly related to and recruited from each area of specialty in the firm.

	3'	5'
	4	3 44
	9	6 47
	14	8 50
	18	11 53
	23	14 55
	28	17 58
	32	19 60
	36	22 63
	41	24 66
	45	27 69
	50	30 71
	55	33 74
	59	36 77
	64	39 80
	69	41 83

SELF-ESTEEM

Proper self-esteem is necessary for all who wish to find job or personal success. This attribute is the right quality for true inner peace as well as for success. More and more people have become aware of the importance of the development of self-esteem. Business leaders and employers offer courses to help their employees attain and add self-esteem. A state government has set up a committee to examine the problem and make recommendations for a plan that will be for the enhancement of self-esteem among the citizenry.

One principal problem in trying to achieve proper and required self-esteem is our inability to accept failure. We must realize that every person has known failure and that we all must accept loss. In business and in life in general, it is our reaction to our failures and our sustained efforts to overcome problems that will bring us a good feeling about ourselves. To enhance our strengths and to become happy and successful, we must take the initial steps to build up our own esteem.

	3'	5'
	4	3 43
	9	6 46
	14	8 49
	19	11 52
	24	14 55
	28	17 58
	32	20 61
	35	21 62
	40	24 64
	44	27 67
	49	29 70
	54	32 73
	59	35 76
	63	38 79
	68	41 81

gwam 3' | 1 | 2 | 3 | 4 | 5
5' | 1 | 2 | 3

KEYSTROKING DRILL

Key each line twice; repeat if time permits.   *Line:* 70 characters   *Goal:* Key adjacent-key sequences with continuity; strike precisely each key.

Adjacent Keys

wed red oil error suit copy new same leads report view over asks basis
buy coin art sale points term post trip suits top shop guide herd says
aware union asked knew tried her needs onion adds there join her equip

polio record serve recent sewed hope adored washers aware are returned
reserves stressed quite pleased effort trees sands union freedom freed
were trade seesaw area tired remove drew removed hermit firefly weaver

Copies of the three reports were distributed last week by the manager.
A contract to prepare a modern safety series for tires was considered.
Action was taken by the credit manager to buy equipment and furniture.

---

	gwam	1'	3'

CORPORATE STOCK

	gwam	1'	3'
A corporation may raise money by issuing shares of its capital	13	4	97
stock. When a person purchases the shares of a corporation, the person	27	9	102
is called a shareholder of the company. A shareholder expects to get a	41	14	107
stock certificate which shows on its face the number of shares it rep-	55	18	111
resents. A certificate is registered in the owner's name with the	69	23	116
corporation. When a corporation raises money by issuing stock, it does	83	28	121
not promise the shareholder that the money will be repaid at some later	98	32	125
date. In fact, it does not promise to pay interest. The money that the	112	37	130
corporation realizes from the sale of stock becomes a permanent part of	127	42	135
the corporation. When you buy a share of stock, you own a part of the	141	47	140
company. You will enjoy the right to share in the profits that the com-	155	52	145
pany distributes to its shareholders. These profits are called dividends	170	57	150
and are normally paid quarterly.	176	59	152
An issue of stock is bought normally by an investment banking house.	14	63	156
The banking house sells the shares to individuals at a higher cost. The	29	68	161
par value of a share is a value shown on the certificate. If stock were	43	73	166
issued without giving the shares any value, it has nonpar value. After	58	78	171
an issue of stock has been sold, individuals buy and sell the shares at	72	83	176
any price. This is called market value. The market value depends on	86	87	180
what individuals predict about the future earnings and stability of a	100	92	185
corporation.	102	93	186

gwam	1'	1	2	3	4	5	6	7	8	9	10	11	12	13	14
	3'		1		2		3		4		5				

PYRAMID PARAGRAPHS

Line: 70 characters
Goal: Build speed. Key each line of the paragraph within 15", 12", or 10".

Eliminate waste motion.
Key: 1' timing on the paragraph. If you finish a line before the time in-

terval is called, continue to the next line; if not, repeat the unfinished line.

	gwam 1'
With all habits, good and	5
bad, practice makes the habits	11
an important part of our lives. An	18
essential habit we ought to all practice	26
is thrift. This means that we hold back cer-	35
tain amounts from our payroll every week or month.	45
We then invest these dollars in the type of growth fund	56
which will increase steadily. It is amazing to find how our	68
necessities can become unnecessary. There is also the gratifica-	81
tion that the investment will grow. Open such a thrift plan this day.	95

gwam 1' | 1 | 2 | 3 | 4 | 5 | 6 | 7 | 8 | 9 | 10 | 11 | 12 | 13 | 14 |

---

	gwam 1'	3'
CINCO DE MAYO Cinco de Mayo is one of Mexico's most important holidays. It is a	13	4 49
day that commemorates the victory over the French forces at Puebla on	27	9 54
the fifth day of May. This special day is celebrated in all parts of	41	14 59
the country and in other nations where there is a Hispanic population.	56	19 63
The day will usually start with a beautiful parade, and one will often	70	23 68
see people wearing quaint national costumes of their land. Excellent	84	28 73
food and beverages are served, and sometimes important people give	97	32 77
speeches. Later in the day, people join in the happy dancing; and, of	112	37 82
course, fireworks bring the evening to a close. It is a day of pleasure	126	42 87
and a symbol of freedom for all citizens.	134	45 90

	gwam 1'	3'
UTOPIA A utopian may be said to be a dreamer who urges impractical reforms	14	4 50
or who expects a unique state of perfection in the world. An ideal	27	9 55
society has often been described by those who were living in times of	41	14 60
great problems. Some of the major ideas which they set forth have in-	55	18 64
cluded shorter work hours, medical aid, free education, and freedom	69	23 69
for all. Much progress has been made over the last century, and the	83	27 73
utopian dream is somewhat closer. Yet, there is still much to do in	96	32 78
order to eliminate prejudice, poverty, and pollution, to name only three	111	37 83
of our present ills. A better society will only be realized through the	126	42 88
work of many people of good will, integrity, and compassion.	138	46 92

gwam 1' | 1 | 2 | 3 | 4 | 5 | 6 | 7 | 8 | 9 | 10 | 11 | 12 | 13 | 14 |
3' | 1 | 2 | 3 | 4 | 5 |

GOOD OFFICE PROCEDURES

	gwam	3'	5'
A business must use good office procedures if it is to control its	5	3	86
costs and sustain an even flow of work. In the office word processing	9	6	89
center, some basic procedures lend themselves to cost and flow of work	14	8	92
control. Workers log or record a job from its entry into the center	19	11	95
to its final exit. The log serves several purposes for the supervisor	23	14	98
responsible for cost and work control. If a document's status is in	28	17	100
question, it can be traced on the log sheet. The supervisor can use the	33	20	103
log to determine turnaround time and to measure work, too. The super-	37	23	106
visor checks work to evaluate productivity, to become aware of likely	42	25	109
problems, and to decide if more training or extra staff are needed.	47	28	112
There are more procedures which can help a supervisor to control	51	30	114
costs and to keep the flow of work even. Establishing priorities for	56	33	117
workers means that they will know to do the most urgent work first.	60	36	120
Setting time goals for finishing certain tasks encourages the staff to	65	39	123
provide prompt service to those who need work done. Using a standard	70	42	125
format for letters, reports, and other documents reduces errors, saves	74	45	128
time for the staff, and simplifies the training of new personnel. The	79	47	131
supervisor should see that the rules are written down in a manual for	84	50	134
workers to use. A procedures manual helps workers to learn to do their	89	53	137
work easily and assures that the work they put out is of high quality.	93	56	140
For routine letters or for repetitive paragraphs to be used in	98	59	142
letters or reports, it is useful to develop and use standard material	102	61	145
that employees understand is to be used in every appropriate case. Each	107	64	148
one of these items should be assigned a code number so that it can be	112	67	151
filed and retrieved easily. The codes are given in the procedures manu-	117	70	154
als so that both the authors who originate the work and the workers who	121	73	156
will produce it can insert the material when applicable. In-house train-	126	76	159
ing can serve to teach all who will need to know about the procedures	131	79	162
of the word processing center. Establishing and using the procedures	136	81	165
can help control costs and sustain an even flow of work.	139	84	167

gwam 3' | 1 | 2 | 3 | 4 | 5 |
5' | 1 | 2 | 3 |

	gwam	3'	5'

WALKING

Walking is one of the best ways to keep in shape. It can be done just about anywhere, at any time of the day; and it is one of the few forms of physical exercise that does not require the purchase of special equipment. Daily walking results in stronger muscles, increased lung capacity, and better circulation. In addition, this form of exercise helps the body to reach and maintain a good weight. Finally, regular walking relieves boredom and provides an easy and pleasant way to work off nervous energy.

gwam	3'	5'
4	3	42
9	5	44
14	8	47
19	11	50
23	14	53
28	17	56
33	19	58
34	20	59

Walking need not be a strenuous activity. Elderly people and those with heart problems can safely take lazy strolls for short distances until they are able to build endurance. On the other hand, people who are strong and in good health can walk just as vigorously as they wish without doing the damage to their knees and feet that such activities as running and tennis can cause. Walking is one way that nearly everyone can experience the benefits of regular exercises.

gwam	3'	5'
39	23	62
43	26	65
48	29	68
53	31	70
58	34	73
62	37	76
66	39	78

	gwam	3'	5'

WILLPOWER

Willpower is a strong sense of determination to achieve our goals, no matter what problems we may face. Some people insist that they possess little or no willpower, but this is not the case. Every one of us has the ability to persevere at difficult tasks, even though the effort appears to be more painful for some of us than it is for others. Willpower, when it is accompanied by a fervent desire for success, can enable us to accomplish things that are extremely difficult for most people, such as sticking to a very strict diet.

gwam	3'	5'
4	3	43
9	6	46
14	8	48
19	11	51
23	14	54
28	17	57
33	20	60
36	21	61

Willpower is not only helpful to us when we want to lose weight or to break bad habits; it can also be a considerable aid in reaching our career goals. Willpower enables us to apply all our available physical and mental energy to the performance of our jobs, in spite of any obstacles we may face. It is important to realize that success quite often results from a firm determination to keep trying, even when things are not going particularly well.

gwam	3'	5'
40	24	64
45	27	67
50	30	70
54	33	73
59	36	76
64	38	78
66	40	80

gwam	3'	1	2	3	4	5
	5'	1		2		3

PYRAMID PARAGRAPHS

Line: 70 characters
Goal: Build speed. Key each line of the paragraph within 15", 12", or 10".

Strive to key each line within the time limit. Repeat the goal for the second paragraph.

Key: 1' timing on each paragraph. If you finish a line before the time interval is called, continue to the next line; if not, repeat the unfinished line.

	gwam 1'
Do you display high levels of Type A (coronary	9
prone) behavior patterns? If so, your behavior is	19
characterized by competitiveness and need for achieve-	30
ment, aggression, impatience, and hostility. You also are	41
always under time pressure. Type A people seek out challenges	53
in their environments. During these challenges, Type A people are	66
more hostile and impatient. Such challenges irritate heart disorders.	80
Type A people have a tendency to be unaware of	9
their physical condition and deny health problems,	19
fatigue, and emotions. They do not consult physicians	30
regularly. They tend not to share their personal concerns	41
with others. Type A people tend to struggle hardest in situa-	53
tions where they have the opportunity to gain control. It is rare	66
for Type A people to relax and enjoy the pleasures of a job well done.	80

gwam 1' | 1 | 2 | 3 | 4 | 5 | 6 | 7 | 8 | 9 | 10 | 11 | 12 | 13 | 14 |

OFFICE AUTOMATION

	gwam 1'	3'
Office automation has grown to include such applications as word	13	4 / 91
processing and electronic mail. Electronic mail is a name for a system	27	9 / 96
that is based on a central computer with personal computers attached	41	14 / 101
to the main computer. It permits users to send, store, and receive mes-	56	18 / 106
sages. Also, messages can be sent electronically through space or over	70	23 / 110
the telephone lines. The message is kept in the form of electronic sig-	84	28 / 115
nals until it needs to be changed to a paper copy. This form of mail	98	33 / 120
will permit offices all over the world to be linked. This could be	112	37 / 124
only a one-way communication; or if you wish, you can conduct a two-way	126	42 / 129
conversation with someone as you send messages back and forth.	139	46 / 133
Depending on the software used, several options can be used in	13	50 / 137
sending mail. If you just want anyone in the firm with a terminal to	27	55 / 142
read the message, it is placed on an electronic bulletin board. If you	41	60 / 147
want to receive a confirmation when the recipient reads the message, it	55	65 / 152
can be sent as registered mail. If you expect only one recipient to	69	69 / 156
receive the message, send it as private mail. There are quite a few	83	74 / 161
machines and processes that are utilized for electronic mail. Some	100	78 / 165
types of electronic systems include the use of facsimiles and mailgrams.	111	83 / 170
Many forms of electronic mail will be used in the future.	122	87 / 174

gwam 1' | 1 | 2 | 3 | 4 | 5 | 6 | 7 | 8 | 9 | 10 | 11 | 12 | 13 | 14 |
3' | 1 | 2 | 3 | 4 | 5 |

KEYSTROKING DRILL

Key the entire drill once; repeat if time permits.   *Line:* 70 characters   *Goal:* Key double-letter and one-hand words at the stroke or word level; think the phrase as you key the last three lines.

Double-Letter Words

all free too feel will three book fill less shall bill need full steel
flee issue offer small look mill lass smooth seek took meek jeep still
good fleece spleen aardvark little inn accept droop assess runner thee

One-Hand Words

base my up set are sat in my mull crab after pop kill no you card case
gas were grass sass ware tare gaze cast car care dad sad secede red we
test rate pump plump extra union rat jolly my on read jump hump as few

Common Phrases

to do the | she may | and for | to do it | if he | of us | see you | if he | sound off
run for | thank you for it | may as well | you were | will not go | she gave him
for it may | will do | for us | seems as if | if he will | if they | she has | to it

---

	gwam	1'	3'
JAZZ			

	gwam	1'	3'
Jazz music began in the southern part of our country as a form of	13	4	50
early folk music; but, it was soon appreciated all over the world as the	28	9	55
fascination for this style increased. Throughout most of its history,	42	14	60
its complex rhythm has been characterized by a basic movement or riff.	56	19	65
Improvisation is then added to the basic movement. When two or more	70	23	69
people perform, they improvise as they go along, guided by what they	84	28	74
feel. The blue note, or unexpected flat note, is characteristic of this	99	33	79
music style. Ragtime and dixieland, built from rags and marches, are	113	37	84
both forms of this music style. Because jazz is becoming more popular	127	42	88
each year with music buffs, more festivals are being held.	138	46	92

	gwam	1'	3'
ANNOYING SPEAKERS			

	gwam	1'	3'
Have you had the unnerving experience in which a speaker asks a	13	4	47
question and then either completely ignores your reply or begins a new	27	9	52
subject in the middle of your answer? What about the speaker who takes	41	14	56
a very long pause between each sentence? There is also the person who	56	19	61
thinks the more important the idea, the louder he or she must talk. This	70	23	66
person deserves to spend many hours with a mumbler. Have you ever had	85	28	71
to listen to a person who talked down to the audience or who used mainly	99	33	76
technical jargon or nuances as if the audience understood them? Why is	114	38	80
it that nearly everyone has these or similar eccentricities except us?	128	43	85

gwam	1'	1	2	3	4	5	6	7	8	9	10	11	12	13	14
	3'		1			2			3			4			5	

EMPLOYMENT

Most people hold jobs during at least part of their adult lives, and many have to work continually from late adolescence to or even beyond retirement age. People secure employment for a wide variety of reasons, the most obvious of which is the need or desire to earn money. Very few persons could work for long at a job that did not offer them a means of supporting themselves and their families. But it is also true that few individuals would prefer to spend their lives doing work from which they derive no pleasure and little self-respect. Income and job satisfaction, then, are two very significant factors in how workers regard their jobs and even themselves.

Income is the monetary compensation a worker receives in return for labor. A person's income reflects, among other things, the value to the employer of that person's training, experience, and skill in doing a specific job. Income is also the basis on which a family must organize its standard of living. An adequate salary must provide for all of a family's needs and, preferably, for at least a few of the special items that family members want. In addition, the worker must feel that he or she is paid fairly for the job and that there is a good chance that the salary will grow as the employee gains experience and becomes able to assume more responsibility.

It is easy to see how income is related to job satisfaction. A person who is unable to earn enough money to meet basic expenses feels frustrated, no matter how pleasant the job may be. Similarly, a person who does not receive as much money as do others who perform comparable work is likely to become angry with management. However, income is not the only factor involved in job satisfaction. An enjoyable career is one that uses the worker's skills and provides an opportunity for growth, without demanding more time and effort than the worker is willing or able to devote to it. Both the salary and the work itself should be carefully matched to the employee's needs.

gwam 3'	5'	
4	3	82
9	5	85
14	8	88
18	11	91
23	14	94
28	17	96
32	19	99
37	22	102
41	25	105
45	27	106
49	29	109
54	32	112
59	35	115
63	38	118
68	41	121
73	44	123
78	47	126
83	49	129
87	52	132
89	53	133
93	56	136
98	59	139
103	62	141
108	64	144
112	67	147
117	70	150
122	73	153
125	76	155
130	79	158
133	80	159

gwam 3' | 1 | 2 | 3 | 4 | 5 |
5' | 1 | 2 | 3 |

BAJA CALIFORNIA

The settling of the far-western portion of this nation began in the | 4 | 3 | 48
early part of the seventeen hundreds in a part of Mexico known as Baja | 9 | 6 | 51
California. This peninsula is a long and narrow piece of land running | 14 | 8 | 54
about one thousand miles north and south. The first attempt at settle- | 19 | 11 | 56
ment was probably in the south and gradually, with great effort, moved | 23 | 14 | 59
north through a mission system of expansion. The area still has a few | 28 | 17 | 62
people with most of them living in the north or the extreme southern | 33 | 20 | 65
portion. The weather is quite hot, and there is very little rainfall; | 37 | 22 | 68
this does not allow a good chance for crop growth. Some cattle are | 42 | 25 | 70
found, grain is grown, and there is some mining. Almost every type of | 47 | 28 | 73
desert plant is found here. In the last few decades, some areas have | 51 | 31 | 76
become known as vacation centers. Deep sea fishing has brought attention | 56 | 34 | 79
to the western side of the peninsula. Unfortunately, the real natives of | 61 | 37 | 82
this land have greatly decreased in size due to the inability to live | 66 | 40 | 85
with diseases brought by immigrants. However, the blood of the ancient | 71 | 43 | 88
tribes still flows in the veins of many Baja Californians of today. | 75 | 45 | 90

FELT

One of the oldest types of fabric in the world has been in use for | 4 | 3 | 46
over three thousand years. This fabric, felt, was made for years in a | 9 | 5 | 49
very simple manner. A fiber, usually wool, was washed and spread out. | 14 | 8 | 52
Water and whey were applied. It was then beaten with a club or rolled | 19 | 11 | 55
in a heavy material and pounded. What actually happened in the process | 23 | 14 | 58
was that the wool or other fiber interlocked strands through the mois- | 28 | 17 | 61
ture, heat, agitation, and pressure to develop into a heavy cloth. The | 33 | 20 | 64
procedure today is far more complicated and is performed quickly. How- | 38 | 23 | 66
ever, the principle is very similar. There are now far more than a hun- | 42 | 25 | 69
dred types of felt used in headgear, insulation, packaging, trimming | 47 | 28 | 72
material, and various types of covers. The size and the weight of the | 52 | 31 | 75
fabric varies greatly from three ounces to sixty-five pounds per square | 57 | 34 | 78
yard. The use and areas covered dictates the weight that is selected. | 61 | 37 | 81
Felt, which was commonly used as a grave lining over two thousand years | 66 | 40 | 83
ago, is now seen in just about every society and can be made to repel | 71 | 43 | 86
water, insects, and even fire. | 73 | 44 | 87

gwam 3'   1   2   3   4   5
      5'   1   2   3

KEYSTROKING DRILL

Key each line twice; slowly, then faster.

Line: 70 characters
Goal: Move the fourth finger to the

shift key smoothly, hold firmly, and release quickly.

Left Shift Key

Henry Yates Hilton Head Union Pacific Oak Hill Olivetti Jamiaca Pisces Louisiana Monday Nassau Oregon Nevada Yalta Indiana Louisiana Portland James, Pauline, and Mia will leave for Massachusetts on Monday.

Right Shift Key

Tuesday Friday April Cancer Black Sea Doris Trelles California Emogene Red River Valley Seattle Tennessee Dwight Eisenhower David Copperfield Willie and Saddie left with George and Carol for Gainesville, Florida.

CAPS Lock

IBM Corporation GONE WITH THE WIND dBASE IV EBCDIC NBC ABC LOTUS 1-2-3 CENTURY 21 COBOL and FORTRAN DBA Degree ZIP and OCR TWA Flight 86 FBLA Joe and Sandra read LITTLE WOMEN, TREASURE ISLAND, and ABOU BEN ADHEM.

---

		gwam	1'	3'
INFLATION	Inflation deals with changes in the level of prices rather than in	13	4	89
	employment and output. The term inflation means a rise in the general	28	9	93
	price level. To get a measure of the price level, economists select a	42	14	98
	market basket of goods and develop a price index. Inflation, then, can	56	19	103
	be measured in terms of the producer price index, the consumer price	70	23	108
	index, or the gross national product price deflator. From time to time,	85	29	112
	a situation may cause the general price level to go down. If so, this	99	33	117
	condition is known as deflation.	105	35	119
	There have been many reasons given for the causes of inflation. One	14	40	124
	of the reasons is that a spending unit in the economy tries to buy more	28	44	129
	than the economy can produce. As a result, prices rise. The federal	42	49	133
	deficit can contribute to inflation if the Federal Reserve System in-	56	54	138
	creases the money supply to keep the interest rate down. Another reason	71	59	143
	for inflation may be the labor groups who push up prices. Higher prices	85	63	147
	may just force workers to request higher wages, too. If they get the	99	68	152
	higher wages, producers try to recover with higher prices. When the	113	72	157
	money supply grows faster than the growth in the gross national product,	128	78	162
	higher prices are realized. The supply of money must grow faster than	142	82	167
	the increase in real output.	148	84	168

gwam 1' | 1 | 2 | 3 | 4 | 5 | 6 | 7 | 8 | 9 | 10 | 11 | 12 | 13 | 14 |
      3' | 1 | | 2 | | 3 | | 4 | | 5 |

GUIDED WRITING SENTENCES

Line: 70 characters
Goal: Build speed. Key each sentence in 12" or 10".

Key: 30" or 1' timings on the sentences. If you finish a sentence before the time interval is called, go to the next sentence. For each new timing, continue from last complete sentence keyed.

		gwam per line	12"	10"
1	Penmanship is a lost art.		25	30
2	He or she will go to the city.		30	36
3	Time will prove that all will fall.		35	42
4	Kennels will house both the cat and dog.		40	48
5	Carbon paper still has many uses in business.		45	52
6	Getting back up is just as important as your fall.		50	60
7	Her patchwork quilt won the prize at the local contest.		55	66
8	The power of positive thinking can never be stressed enough.		60	72
9	Her stories were boring to all who were assembled except herself.		65	78
10	If you remain on your toes, it is not easy for others to step on them.		70	84

gwam 1'	1	2	3	4	5	6	7	8	9	10	11	12	13	14
30"	2	4	6	8	10	12	14	16	18	20	22	24	26	28

---

	gwam	1'	3'

RAINBOWS

How many times have you seen ribbons of color appear in the air [13] [4|46] above you? This was likely a rainbow, a series of colors observable [27] [9|51] when falling water droplets are illuminated by a strong light source [40] [13|55] such as the sun. The water droplets, made up of rain or spray from some [55] [18|60] water source, refract the light source into red, orange, yellow, green, [69] [23|65] blue, indigo, and violet colors. The order in which each color appears [84] [28|70] in the rainbow is always determined by its place in the color spectrum, [98] [33|75] from violet on the inside to red on the outside. A secondary rainbow [112] [37|79] sometimes appears above the first, its color series in reversed order. [126] [42|84]

	gwam	1'	3'

PRETZELS

The pretzel came to this country very early, possibly on the first [13] [4|51] ship. The natives took advantage of the opportunity to learn about this [28] [9|55] new food. They would pay or trade just about anything for pretzels. [42] [14|60] Pretzels, which are usually hard and brittle, are made by molding a [56] [18|65] slender roll of dough which is covered with a large amount of salt. They [70] [23|70] are then baked in the figure of a loosened knot. Another form results [85] [28|74] when they are biscuits baked in the shape of crossed arms. The taste is [99] [33|79] excellent and, like peanuts, it is almost impossible to quit eating them [114] [38|84] once you begin. They are usually not a health food, since most avail- [128] [43|89] able pretzels have a considerable quantity of sodium. [138] [46|92]

gwam 1'	1	2	3	4	5	6	7	8	9	10	11	12	13	14
3'		1		2		3		4		5				

LEARNING TO READ

It is essential now for all our youth to do their best to develop | 4 | 3 | 78
their reading vocabulary and to improve their fundamental reading abil- | 9 | 5 | 81
ities. While they are attending school, it appears that young people | 14 | 8 | 84
have no more vital concern than to learn to read with comprehension. | 18 | 11 | 87
This is valid, first of all, because news concerning most of the urgent | 23 | 14 | 90
events on this planet is gained by reading about these events in some | 28 | 17 | 92
written form. If people do not read and comprehend what they have read, | 33 | 20 | 95
the vast amounts of knowledge in areas that are scientific and practical, | 38 | 23 | 98
as well as in political and moral matters, will be literally closed books | 43 | 26 | 101
to them. | 43 | 26 | 102

A school recognizes the importance of reading. In the early grades, | 48 | 29 | 104
reading uses a big portion of time spent by the student and teacher. | 52 | 31 | 107
Reading is a continuing process that young people must cherish through | 57 | 34 | 110
both high school and college, if they choose to go far and be content | 62 | 37 | 113
in life after school. As they grow older, erudite, and wiser, they gain | 67 | 40 | 116
the ability to comprehend ideas that were meaningless in their earlier | 71 | 43 | 119
years. It has been learned that the best way of improving reading power | 76 | 46 | 121
is through the study of vocabulary. If students can just acquire a more | 81 | 49 | 124
extensive vocabulary, they will have the power to enrich old words with | 86 | 52 | 127
new meanings. | 87 | 52 | 128

Reading skill, even though important, is not the only aim of school | 91 | 55 | 131
reading. Quite as essential is the development of appreciation and taste | 96 | 58 | 133
for good literature. The reading which young people do in school will | 101 | 61 | 136
train them to make wise and useful choices when they come to select their | 106 | 64 | 139
own readings. They develop a power and a desire to recognize and react | 111 | 67 | 142
to the better and more useful material. They should be able to carry | 116 | 69 | 145
over to the activities of daily life an ability to read. Understanding, | 120 | 72 | 148
appreciation, and taste may be assumed as the primary ends to be attained | 125 | 75 | 151
by reading. | 126 | 76 | 151

GYPSIES

What is known of this group of people who for many generations | 4 | 3 | 47
have been feared or ignored; and above all, still remain mysterious? | 9 | 5 | 50
For many years, they have been on the move. Their language is formal, a | 14 | 8 | 53
union of the tongues of the nations visited and their ancient Romany | 18 | 11 | 55
dialect. In addition to being peddlers, they have developed skills in | 23 | 14 | 58
dance, animal training, music, and magic. Some were put to death just | 28 | 17 | 61
for being gypsies. Others were made to assimilate but were banned from | 33 | 20 | 64
being in public or religious office in many parts of the world. | 37 | 22 | 66

Evidence of their origin is not clear. The first may have come to | 41 | 25 | 69
Europe from India; others may have been early Christians from Egypt. | 46 | 28 | 72
Gypsies may have no stable habits; they rest if tired or eat if hungry | 51 | 30 | 75
with no regard for time. As many as six million are probably in the | 55 | 33 | 77
world; most continue to travel. Churches and governments have estab- | 60 | 36 | 80
lished schools for the children, and the number who stopped vagabond- | 65 | 39 | 83
ism and now live in major cities has expanded. After years of mobile | 68 | 42 | 86
life, they may quickly realize that their nomadic ways are now in danger. | 73 | 44 | 89

RECREATION EMPLOYMENT

Recreation offers much in the way of employment to young people on | 4 | 3 | 47
either a part- or full-time basis or on a temporary or permanent basis. | 9 | 6 | 50
As we live longer and have more hours of leisure time, the need for | 14 | 8 | 53
professional assistance, supervision, and counsel grows. People on | 18 | 11 | 56
vacation, just enjoying a pastime, or in retirement still prefer an | 23 | 14 | 58
environment that will allow the best use of time and money. | 27 | 16 | 61

A hotel, motel, camp, or lodge may require competent help in host- | 31 | 19 | 63
ing tourists. The number of people needed is also increasing in travel | 36 | 22 | 66
agencies; more tour directors and guides are required. Sports and health | 41 | 25 | 69
clubs catering to any age are on the increase. As with any job, the | 46 | 27 | 72
better prepared you are, the better your chances of success. Patience, | 50 | 30 | 75
a good attitude, and respect for others are needed. For a position in a | 55 | 33 | 78
new area, knowledge of a foreign language and the willingness to study | 60 | 36 | 81
and learn the local history and geography will realize big dividends. | 65 | 39 | 83
One of the positive aspects of this type of work is that the customers | 69 | 42 | 86
are relaxed and usually in a good frame of mind. This can be catching. | 74 | 45 | 89

gwam 3' | 1 | 2 | 3 | 4 | 5
5' | 1 | 2 | 3

PYRAMID PARAGRAPHS

Line: 70 characters
Goal: Build speed. Key each line of the paragraph within 15", 12", or 10".

Strive to key each line within the time limit. Repeat the goal for the second paragraph.

Key: 1' timing on the paragraph. If you finish a line before the time interval is called, continue to the next line; if not, repeat the unfinished line.

	gwam 1'
Controlling the spiraling costs of health care	9
benefits will become a major task of corporations.	19
Keeping job satisfaction high among young employees so	30
that they will not leave also will have an effect on costs	41
and productivity. To help with this problem, employee fitness	53
programs have been created by corporations. Benefits include less	66
absenteeism, fewer on-the-job injuries, and reduced health care costs.	80
During the past few years, a number of studies	9
have suggested that fitness programs increase pro-	19
ductivity in mentally stressful jobs. Current studies	30
found that absenteeism was reduced after the initiation of	41
a fitness program. Participants in such programs were usually	53
more conscientious employees. Higher insurance premiums, illness,	66
and absenteeism could have a severe financial effect on a corporation.	80

gwam 1' | 1 | 2 | 3 | 4 | 5 | 6 | 7 | 8 | 9 | 10 | 11 | 12 | 13 | 14 |

U. S. MONEY

	gwam 1'	3'
The use of money is something that people in each society accept.	13	4
Today, most nations use fiat money as their medium of exchange. This	27	9
means money by government decree. There are many different forms of	41	14
money in the United States. Of these, however, the most familiar are	55	18
coins and currency. The term coin refers to metallic forms of money.	69	23
The term currency refers to paper money issued by the government through	84	28
an act of law. The coins of the United States come in six denomina-	98	32
tions, starting with the penny and ranging up to the dollar. The actual	112	37
value of the metal making up each coin today is only a fraction of the	126	42
coin's face value. All the currency of the United States is issued by	141	47
the Federal Reserve System, which is a central banking institution owned	155	52
by banks and operated in the public interest.	164	55
One of the other forms of money is demand deposits. This refers to	14	59
deposits available on demand at certain banks. These deposits are avail-	28	64
able whenever the depositor desires to have them. A check is used to	42	69
withdraw money from these funds. A bank receives no preliminary notice	57	74
from the depositor that the money will be removed. The bank just learns	71	78
this when the check arrives to be cashed. Two other forms of money are	86	83
savings and time deposits. These types of deposits cannot be withdrawn	100	88
quickly by check. Money will continue to change in shape and size in the	115	93
future. There may be a time when plastic cards and computer transactions	130	98
are the primary means of exchange.	136	100

gwam 1' | 1 | 2 | 3 | 4 | 5 | 6 | 7 | 8 | 9 | 10 | 11 | 12 | 13 | 14 |
3' | 1 | 2 | 3 | 4 | 5 |

PYRAMID PARAGRAPHS

Line: 70 characters
Goal: Build speed. Key each line of the paragraph within 15", 12", or 10".

Return without looking at copy.
Key: 1' timing on the paragraph. If you finish a line before the time

interval is called, continue to the next line; if not, repeat the unfinished line.

	gwam 1'
People must learn to live	5
with others because we need to	11
be gregarious. A man or woman will	18
not remain aloof from the experiences of	26
others. The chances of a person becoming the	35
hermit or recluse of old are very remote. Does it	45
mean that we must go through life totally engulfed by a	56
crowd of humans and humanoids? No, we require the peace and	68
solitude needed to let the tensions drain. Even reverie might be	81
necessary for the benefit of our own anatomical and mental well-being.	95

gwam 1' | 1 | 2 | 3 | 4 | 5 | 6 | 7 | 8 | 9 | 10 | 11 | 12 | 13 | 14 |

WEIGHT CONTROL

	gwam 1'	3'
One of the most popular activities among all age groups of the	13	4 51
current population is weight control. The words, weight control, will	27	9 56
just about always signify loss of size or of weight. In many such pro-	41	14 60
grams, you will receive advice, an exercise regimen, and often a require-	56	18 65
ment to buy a certain brand of foods. The programs sound so easy that	70	23 70
one expects a new, fun hobby rather than a rigid, painful agenda. No	84	28 75
doubt many can profit from such plans, but the record of success usually	98	33 80
does not justify the extreme claims some programs make. Common sense	112	37 84
will tell us that the emphasis should be on eating healthy food to live	127	42 89
better, not on living so we can eat tasty food of questionable merit.	141	47 94

DEJA VU

	gwam 1'	3'
You enter a room in a strange building for the first time, but an	13	4 51
eerie feeling reminds you that you have been there before. You meet	27	9 56
someone for the first time, but the exchange of pleasantries is very	41	14 60
familiar. Your new acquaintance assures you that the two of you have	55	18 65
never met before. Why does this situation take place? There is no	68	23 69
absolute answer, but this phenomenon occurs often enough to have been	82	27 74
given a name. It is called deja vu, which is defined as something	96	32 79
familiar or an illusion of recognizing events that were never actually	110	37 83
experienced before. The next time you have this sensation, ask yourself	125	41 88
if the scenario could have been identical, but you could have been	138	46 93
different.	140	47 93

gwam 1' | 1 | 2 | 3 | 4 | 5 | 6 | 7 | 8 | 9 | 10 | 11 | 12 | 13 | 14 |
3' | 1 | | 2 | | 3 | | 4 | | 5 |

A SENSE OF HUMOR

A sense of humor is one of the most valuable characteristics we can have when it comes to understanding and getting along with other people. There is nothing like a good joke to ease difficult encounters and to relieve the strain of modern life. Further, the ability to see the funny side of daily affairs and of our own actions is a sign of physical and mental health. However, not all of us possess a highly developed sense of humor. Although nearly everyone enjoys laughing and being amused, people differ widely in their capacity to appreciate and to accept humor. Many people are unable under any condition to see the humor in any matter having to do with themselves.

A number of research studies have shown that a good sense of humor is an expression of intelligence. Persons who make high scores on intelligence tests also tend to show more than ordinary ability to see the funny side of things. In addition, students who are very witty and show great ability to appreciate humorous situations make higher grades in their school work and appear to get quite a bit more pleasure and satisfaction out of their lives than do students who are less sensitive to humor. Very bright individuals are capable of seeing circumstances from more than one point of view, and they seem to realize that few things in life are so serious that they are not open to humor.

A well-developed sense of humor appears to go hand in hand with a well-balanced personality. Emotionally healthy people tend to respond at once to the humor in jokes, cartoons, and daily situations. These people seem to have the ability to discern what others are feeling and to look at the world, and even at themselves, through the eyes of other persons. Well-adjusted people are those who have developed a sense of perspective that keeps them from seeing things as more important than they truly are. They are able to place enough distance between themselves and things that make them unhappy or anxious that they can laugh at these situations and begin to deal with them effectively.

	3'	5'
	5	3	85
	9	6	88
	14	9	91
	19	11	94
	24	14	97
	29	17	100
	33	20	103
	38	23	106
	43	26	108
	45	27	110
	50	30	113
	55	33	115
	59	36	118
	64	38	121
	69	41	124
	74	44	127
	78	47	130
	83	50	133
	88	53	135
	91	55	138
	96	57	140
	101	60	143
	105	63	146
	110	66	149
	115	69	152
	120	72	154
	125	75	157
	129	77	160
	134	80	163
	138	83	165

gwam 3' | 1 | 2 | 3 | 4 | 5 |
5' | 1 | 2 | 3 |

LEASING

	gwam 3'	5'
The high cost of running a business in a competitive market has a	4	3	76
great influence on how a company will acquire its office equipment, such	9	6	79
as computers, printers, fax machines, copiers, and word processors.	14	8	81
Years ago, when a firm had to acquire new equipment, they faced only	18	11	84
two choices. The firm wrote a check to the seller, or the buyer went	23	14	87
to a bank for a loan. In the turbulent economic times of today, fewer	28	17	90
companies have found that paying cash for their equipment is the best	33	19	93
route. Cash is judged to be one of the most precious commodities in	37	22	95
any business venture. It is best preserved for product development and	42	25	98
marketing, for expansion into other markets, or for worker training and	47	28	101
development. In other words, cash is best invested in a project that	51	31	104
will provide a healthy return. The usual bank financing of office equip-	56	34	107
ment also has a downside. Large- or small-size firms like to keep the	61	37	110
bank credit lines open for unforeseen needs. Banks are often not re-	66	39	112
ceptive to contracts long enough to cut the monthly payments down to a	70	42	114
reasonable level.	71	43	116

The high cost of running a business in a competitive market has a great influence on how a company will acquire its office equipment, such as computers, printers, fax machines, copiers, and word processors. Years ago, when a firm had to acquire new equipment, they faced only two choices. The firm wrote a check to the seller, or the buyer went to a bank for a loan. In the turbulent economic times of today, fewer companies have found that paying cash for their equipment is the best route. Cash is judged to be one of the most precious commodities in any business venture. It is best preserved for product development and marketing, for expansion into other markets, or for worker training and development. In other words, cash is best invested in a project that will provide a healthy return. The usual bank financing of office equipment also has a downside. Large- or small-size firms like to keep the bank credit lines open for unforeseen needs. Banks are often not receptive to contracts long enough to cut the monthly payments down to a reasonable level.

	gwam 3'	5'
More and more companies are now turning to a lease to obtain most	76	46	118
of their office equipment. Leasing will save cash, since the entire cost	81	48	122
can be financed. Lease terms may go as long as five or six years to keep	86	51	125
the payments as low as possible. Leasing can lower taxable income as a	91	54	127
lease may be treated as a deductible operating expense. With cash pur-	95	57	130
chases or bank loans, a firm can only depreciate the equipment, usually a	100	60	133
long-time write off. Leases will allow companies to upgrade during the	105	63	136
life of a contract. Thus, firms that can lease will always have state-	110	66	139
of-the-art technology. Because the use of equipment, rather than its	114	69	142
ownership, is what will enhance productivity, leasing is a very attrac-	119	71	145
tive option for the businesses of today.	122	73	146

More and more companies are now turning to a lease to obtain most of their office equipment. Leasing will save cash, since the entire cost can be financed. Lease terms may go as long as five or six years to keep the payments as low as possible. Leasing can lower taxable income as a lease may be treated as a deductible operating expense. With cash purchases or bank loans, a firm can only depreciate the equipment, usually a long-time write off. Leases will allow companies to upgrade during the life of a contract. Thus, firms that can lease will always have state-of-the-art technology. Because the use of equipment, rather than its ownership, is what will enhance productivity, leasing is a very attractive option for the businesses of today.

gwam 3' | 1 | 2 | 3 | 4 | 5 |
5' | 1 | 2 | 3 |

		gwam	1'	3'

STEREO SYSTEMS

It is very important that you know enough about audio equipment before you buy a stereo system. A full stereo system usually contains two speakers, a turntable, an amplifier, and a tuner. Less sophisticated systems often combine the latter two items into one piece of equipment called a receiver. You may realize that you are only interested in a compact system. It has two speakers and just one unit that contains a turntable, a receiver, and often a tape deck. A compact system costs less and takes up very little space. Once you have decided which type of system best fits your needs and your budget, listen to as many of these systems as possible. Do not expect to select a system quickly. The manufacturers' specifications can be of help if you learn how to read them. You are the best person who can decide which stereo system has the best sound and which system will best fit your life style.

Line	gwam	1'	3'
1	13	4	65
2	27	9	70
3	41	14	74
4	54	18	79
5	68	23	83
6	82	27	88
7	96	32	93
8	111	37	97
9	125	42	102
10	139	46	107
11	153	51	112
12	167	56	116
13	182	61	121

		gwam	1'	3'

AUTO INSURANCE

There are millions of auto accidents in the United States annually. You need to buy auto insurance and are required by law to buy coverage. Just think each time that you drive you risk an accident that could make you responsible for damages and for other people's lives. All drivers can have accidents. Even though you may be a good driver, the other person involved in the accident may have no money, no insurance, and no driving skills. You do realize that your insurance and your good driving skills will be some protection. Autos cost lots of money and so does having them repaired. As a result, your insurance may be quite expensive. You need to decide what possibilities to cover and the total amount of coverage. Your agent will assist you with your auto insurance needs and can help you make wise decisions about the primary items to include in your automobile policy.

Line	gwam	1'	3'
1	14	5	64
2	28	9	68
3	42	14	73
4	56	18	78
5	70	23	82
6	84	28	87
7	98	33	92
8	112	37	96
9	126	42	101
10	141	47	106
11	154	51	110
12	169	56	115
13	177	59	118

gwam 1' | 1 | 2 | 3 | 4 | 5 | 6 | 7 | 8 | 9 | 10 | 11 | 12 | 13 | 14 |
3' | 1 | 2 | 3 | 4 | 5 |

KEYSTROKING DRILL

Key the entire drill once; repeat if time permits.   *Line:* 70 characters   *Goal:* Maintain a light, careful stroke. Proofread after each series.

Shift Key   Abner, Baker, Croft, Dunn, Elston, Farrell, Grange, Hughes, Ives, Jebb
Kilner, Lamb, Mott, Nevers, Oakson, Paulsen, Quale, Ruston, Shaw, Tubb
Umland, Villavicencio, Weinberg, Xavier, Yamaguchi, Zuniga, Arne, Bach

La Hunh, Nguyen, McCarthy, Van Galder, Xion Xer, Santa Fe, Kuril, Lund
Santa Clara, San Fernando, La Posada, O'Dell, McNamara, Saki, Mon Pere
San Romani, MacDonald, IJssel, La Coruna, O'Higgins, McGlothlin, McGee

Javier and Pam Cadem went through Frontera and Beliz during last June.
John Paul Gleeson flew to Mount Elbert to meet Maria, Lara, and Wayne.
El Cajon is near San Diego; Lydda is in Israel; Lunberg is in Germany.

		gwam	1'	3'
CERAMICS	Nearly all of us at one time or another have had the pleasant expe-	13	4	50
	rience of fashioning moist clay into interesting forms. Ceramics, which	28	9	55
	is the art of making items with clay and glazes, has been practiced for	42	14	60
	many centuries. Its artistic use of shapes, colors, and glazes makes ce-	57	19	65
	ramics one of the most beautiful of all art forms, as well as one of the	72	24	70
	most involved. A ceramist must be able to model clay, harden the result-	86	29	75
	ing item by heating it at a very high temperature, apply paints or other	101	34	80
	decorations, add clear or colored glazes, and fire the item once again.	115	38	84
	It can take an individual many years to develop the skills necessary to	130	43	89
	design a really fine ceramic work of art.	138	46	92

		gwam	1'	3'
THE FUTURE OFFICE	Experts forecasting the office of the future may tell us about a	13	4	47
	number of definite innovations which may change the age-old view and	27	9	52
	customs of the business office. Some supervisors will be elected by	41	13	57
	the workers; not all will be chosen by those in a higher position.	54	18	61
	Heavy phone usage will continue and even increase some, but electronic	68	23	66
	means of communication will grow at a faster rate. Workers will be given	83	28	71
	time off just for the improvement of their mental health. There will	97	32	75
	be a sizable amount of paid work permitted and even encouraged in the	111	37	80
	homes of the workers. The coffee break will be changed to include more	125	42	85
	nutritious liquids.	129	43	86

gwam 1' | 1 | 2 | 3 | 4 | 5 | 6 | 7 | 8 | 9 | 10 | 11 | 12 | 13 | 14 |
3' | 1 | 2 | 3 | 4 | 5 |

MONEY

No matter what its form, money is the medium in which prices are   4 | 3 | 82
stated, debts are paid, and goods and services are exchanged among people   7 | 6 | 85
and nations. Money has changed drastically over the years. History   14 | 8 | 88
shows that many different items have served as money. At one time, for   19 | 11 | 91
example, dried fish, rock salt, shells, tobacco, and stones were all used   24 | 14 | 94
as money. Gold and silver were used the most often. Like other metals,   28 | 17 | 97
they had the advantage of being durable and easy to recognize, as well as   33 | 20 | 100
having a high intrinsic value. Coins were first used about a thousand   38 | 23 | 103
years after society began using metal as money.   41 | 25 | 105

Because coins were convenient, they helped metal money to be ac-   46 | 27 | 107
cepted. However, at first ambitious people often shaved the outside of   50 | 30 | 110
the coins to increase their supply of metal. To stop this, the edges   55 | 33 | 113
were milled so that little ridges existed. As a result, citizens did   60 | 36 | 116
not have to weigh and test these metals before goods were exchanged.   64 | 39 | 119
Approximately three hundred years ago, paper money was introduced. Over   69 | 42 | 121
the years, paper money has lost much of its worth, but gradually people   74 | 44 | 124
have learned how to maintain its value. Consequently, just as money is   79 | 47 | 127
not what it used to be, a dollar is not worth what it used to be.   83 | 50 | 130

Money can be an abstract item rather than a physical item. Checking   88 | 53 | 133
accounts, which are a kind of credit money, account for about three-   92 | 55 | 135
quarters of our total monetary supply, and paper currency and coin make   97 | 58 | 138
up the remainder. Credit cards are now being used far more than demand   102 | 61 | 141
deposits. Some people predict that in a not too distant future we will   107 | 64 | 144
have no need for physical money. The computer is able to do any fiscal   112 | 67 | 147
function with greater rapidity and far more accurately than the conven-   116 | 70 | 150
tional means of handling demand deposits. It is hard to imagine a soci-   121 | 73 | 153
ety with no checks, drafts, coins, or paper money; but many now predict   126 | 76 | 155
that only a lack of public approval stops the computer from becoming the   131 | 78 | 158
major factor in our financial lives.   133 | 80 | 160

gwam 3' | 1 | 2 | 3 | 4 | 5
5' | 1 | 2 | 3

WORLD FOOD SUPPLY

The average food supply in the world depends on many factors. One main factor is land. Only about one-half of the arable land is now in production. However, the land in use is the best. The land remaining will produce but only at a very high cost. Water is yet another factor. Most accessible water has already been tapped. Sea water is plentiful, but it must be processed and transported to be fit for use. This is expensive. Fertilizer will increase food production but is not always accessible. Only the wealthy nations can afford fertilizer in the world market. The use of chemicals solves some of the shortage problems by increasing food crops; but in recent years, they have brought us dangerous side effects. Energy in the form of gas, oil, and coal or other minerals needed for farm equipment is costly and is limited in some parts of the globe. Storage of the food supply is a problem, and unlike some items which can be stored for a long time, food items spoil quickly.

Disasters such as droughts, blights, erosion, and floods will occur in spite of our very best plans and efforts. Such enigmas cannot be avoided, but human assistance can reduce them. Changes in eating practices will benefit our food supply. Eight pounds of grain are needed for a single pound of meat. This quantity of grain will provide food for one person for a week. The poor nations usually maintain and even increase their birth rates. The numbers are expanding on a worldwide basis. A lower birth rate will mitigate food problems in many crowded nations. Although many nations try to be self-sufficient in food production and many are in part successful, additional free trade and better cooperation will benefit all. There is wastage in all links in a food chain, but the loss is far too great. Reducing such waste is a need which can be reached by the use of good judgment and serious effort.

gwam 3' | 1 | 2 | 3 | 4 | 5 |
      5' | 1 | 2 | 3 |

KEYSTROKING DRILL

Key the entire drill once; repeat if time permits. *Line:* 70 characters   *Goal:* Think each stroke on the long words; think the entire word on the short ones.

High-Frequency Words—Long

circumstances agreement administration possibility development factory political personnel reading studies transportation division conference shipment yesterday merchandise organizations successful representative

employment invoice maximum responsibility original considerable effort physical forward excellent features approximately apparently afternoon literature following financial exchange circumstances national society

High-Frequency Words—Short

why you yet six the soon son job had go for each eye did city can card up act ago age an all air lot red sure two you well war saw put left a ten tell per on oil its it is one as off fact far any air aid act able

how his felt due fair fact did dead data cost card old met our out own run item it's open or press fit end deal does done but came to side up vote staff this we was wall write over her his how learn let life hand

	gwam	1'	3'

FOG

Fog is often associated with a foghorn giving warning to a moving ship.   Yet as a result of condensation taking place near or at the surface of the ground, fog is also present many miles from any large body of water.   Fog can present travel problems on the water, on the land, and in the air.   An airplane may have little trouble with snow, rain, heat, or cold; however, fog may keep a small plane or even a large, sophisticated jet on the ground.   Fog is also associated with danger and intrigue.   It has set the background for many mystery stories dealing with suspense, vanishing heroines, and the return of the dead.   A shadowy figure moving through a dark, foggy night can become whatever size and shape the imagination will allow it to become.

gwam	1'	3'
13	4	54
27	9	59
42	14	64
56	19	69
70	23	73
83	28	78
97	32	82
111	37	87
125	42	92
139	46	96
150	50	100

HEALTH-CARE EMPLOYMENT

A future in the field of health care will look quite promising for those entering the labor force in the next decade.   The rate of growth in health care will be one of the largest of all occupations.   We may think only of medical doctors and nurses in the healing arts.   Yet, so much emphasis is now being put on keeping healthy, as well as regaining health, that the field has taken additional paths.   Growth fields now include those such as speech and hearing pathology, diet control, physical therapy, and rehabilitation.   Supporting areas, such as word processing, will also realize growth in the health field.   To prepare for a job in this field, one can begin by a study of sciences while in school.

gwam	1'	3'
13	4	52
28	9	57
42	14	61
56	19	66
70	23	71
85	28	76
99	33	80
113	37	85
127	42	90
141	47	94
142	47	95

gwam 1' | 1 | 2 | 3 | 4 | 5 | 6 | 7 | 8 | 9 | 10 | 11 | 12 | 13 | 14 |
3' | | 1 | | 2 | | 3 | | 4 | | 5 |

GUIDED WRITING SENTENCES

Line: 70 characters
Goal: Build speed. Key each sentence in 12" or 10".

Key: 30" or 1' timings on the sentences. If you finish a sentence before the time interval is called, go to the next sentence. For each new timing, continue from last complete sentence keyed.

		gwam per line	12"	10"
1	My choice of fish is cod.		25	30
2	Learn to swim before you dive.		30	36
3	Prize boxes of dates arrived today.		35	42
4	Poor health knows no social constraints.		40	48
5	Always proofread, particularly your own work.		45	52
6	The quickest errors to locate are seldom your own.		50	60
7	He was masterful at distracting the thoughts of others.		55	66
8	Do not overlook the employment contacts of your instructors.		60	72
9	Huge profits will often trigger an investigation and competition.		65	78
10	We appreciate your fine cooperation in reporting an incorrect billing.		70	84

gwam	1'	1	2	3	4	5	6	7	8	9	10	11	12	13	14
	30"	2	4	6	8	10	12	14	16	18	20	22	24	26	28

---

			gwam	1'	3'

CORN

Corn is thought to have originated in the western world, but it is [13] [4] [55]
now found in all areas of the world. It provides food for people and [27] [9] [60]
livestock and is a raw material for industry. It grows especially well [42] [14] [65]
in areas which have a long, hot growing season and abundant rainfall; [56] [19] [69]
therefore, most of the corn in this country is grown in the Midwest. [70] [23] [74]
Corn needs a rich soil, but planting it year after year in the same area [84] [28] [79]
is detrimental to the land because it removes many nutrients from the [98] [33] [84]
ground. Once very susceptible to drought and insects, hybrid types have [113] [38] [89]
been able to cut losses and keep production up. Although these and other [128] [43] [93]
improvements have brought about larger yields, increasing overhead [141] [47] [98]
costs and land values keep production costs of corn high. [153] [51] [102]

			gwam	1'	3'

THE CONSUMER MOVEMENT

The consumer movement has made many of us aware of problems and [13] [4] [50]
ways that we as consumers can receive protection. Over the past years, [27] [9] [55]
many laws have been passed that protect the consumer. These laws center [42] [14] [60]
around the right to security, the right to choose and to be informed, [56] [19] [65]
and the right to be heard. Consumers are protected against the selling [70] [23] [70]
of goods that are dangerous to our safety and health. We have the right [85] [28] [74]
to choose between various goods and services at competitive prices. We [99] [33] [79]
have the right to be told of deceitful practices, and we have the right [114] [38] [84]
to consumer representation in government. As a result of the consumer [128] [43] [89]
movement, our rights have been protected and expanded. [139] [46] [92]

gwam	1'	1	2	3	4	5	6	7	8	9	10	11	12	13	14
	3'		1		2		3		4		5				

CHOICE OF VOCATIONS

Few decisions you make will have a greater impact on your life than | 4 | 3 | 71
your selection of a vocation, the activity which will occupy large por- | 9 | 6 | 74
tions of your waking hours much of your life. First, you should seek a | 14 | 8 | 77
job that you know you will like, one to which you will look forward even | 19 | 11 | 80
early in the morning. While money, fringe benefits, security, and | 23 | 14 | 82
promotions are vital; they are not everything. The satisfaction that | 28 | 17 | 85
comes from labor that makes a positive contribution to society will make | 33 | 20 | 88
you much happier with your career. An environment that allows many | 37 | 22 | 91
opportunities for you to take pride in your work is also desirable. | 42 | 25 | 94

Not all jobs require a college education; yet, the number of jobs | 46 | 28 | 96
requiring some college credits is growing. Staying in school and taking | 51 | 31 | 99
advantage of all your opportunities will always pay well in the long | 56 | 33 | 102
haul. Continuing education has become common today in many fields. | 60 | 36 | 105
Plan to add such a program to your long-range goals. As products and | 65 | 39 | 107
materials change quickly, so do jobs. Those who are eager and willing to | 70 | 42 | 110
keep abreast of the latest advances and change with the times will get | 75 | 45 | 113
the best jobs. | 76 | 46 | 114

We all switch jobs many times during our careers. There is nothing | 80 | 48 | 117
wrong with testing a certain vocation, then going on to something else | 85 | 51 | 119
that appears to have more lasting challenges. However, too many job | 90 | 54 | 122
changes do not look good on a resume. Do not overlook small business | 94 | 57 | 125
opportunities or going into business for yourself. Working for a large- | 99 | 59 | 128
sized firm or for someone else may have disadvantages. Bear in mind | 104 | 62 | 131
that it may be better to be moderately successful in a career you like | 108 | 65 | 133
than to be highly successful in a job filled with constant pressures or | 113 | 68 | 136
unhappiness. | 114 | 68 | 137

		gwam	3'	5'

SUPERSTITIONS

There are very few people who would not admit to having one or | 4 | 3 | 69

two irrational beliefs or superstitions. One person may feel concern | 9 | 5 | 72

about a black cat crossing his or her path. Another person may have to | 14 | 8 | 75

check the horoscope in the paper each day, while yet another person will | 19 | 11 | 78

avidly wish to check with an astrologer. Superstitions are not based | 23 | 14 | 81

on logic but more on personal emotion or cultural conditioning. Although | 28 | 17 | 84

it is easy to dismiss them as absurd, only those who can break a mirror | 33 | 20 | 87

without a second thought are fully entitled to do so. | 37 | 22 | 89

Historically, many superstitions have come from the time of early | 41 | 24 | 91

religions when people worshipped the elements. For example, the import- | 46 | 27 | 94

ance once given to fire and iron has continued today when people carry | 51 | 30 | 97

a piece of coal or a small horseshoe as a good-luck piece. In earlier | 55 | 33 | 100

times, people used to keep their fireplaces going all evening to keep the | 60 | 36 | 103

fairies warm. When moving to a new home, they would often take embers | 65 | 39 | 106

from the old fireplace to burn in their new dwelling. Housewarming par- | 70 | 42 | 108

ties, which occur today, are a result of this old custom. | 73 | 44 | 111

A number of these beliefs are based on positive ideas rather than | 78 | 47 | 113

on simply avoiding bad conditions. Thus, many people believe good luck | 83 | 50 | 116

will follow those who find several four-leaf clovers or who carry a rab- | 88 | 52 | 119

bit's foot. If a person's right ear tingles, perhaps something good is | 93 | 55 | 122

being said about that person. Nothing proves that hanging a horseshoe | 97 | 58 | 125

on a building will bring better times, that eating crusts will result in | 102 | 61 | 128

curly hair, or that rolling an egg across a field will bring a better | 107 | 64 | 131

fall harvest. However, no one said there is any reason to superstitions. | 112 | 67 | 134

gwam	3'	1	2	3	4	5
	5'	1		2		3

PYRAMID PARAGRAPHS

Line: 70 characters
Goal: Build speed. Key each line of the paragraph within 15", 12", or 10".

Keep fingers curved in upright position with finger tips just lightly touching the home keys.

Key: 1' timing on the paragraph. If you finish a line before the time interval is called, continue to the next line; if not, repeat the unfinished line.

	gwam 1'
You have just one pair of	5
eyes, thus extreme care may be	11
your guide. All reading must occur	18
in good light, and glare must be avoided	26
at all times. Reading on the train or in the	35
automobile can also cause discomfort due to motion	45
problems. Watery eyes, swollen eyelids, and immoderate	56
tilting of the head may be the message that a thorough exam-	68
ination is required. Don't take chances with the sense of sight.	84
Your sense of sight is much too valuable to warrant a careless action.	95

gwam 1' | 1 | 2 | 3 | 4 | 5 | 6 | 7 | 8 | 9 | 10 | 11 | 12 | 13 | 14 |

THE HOUSEFLY

	gwam 1'	3'
The common housefly has a well-designed body that is about eight	13	4	55
millimeters long and weighs about thirty milligrams, with a wingspan of	27	9	60
approximately twice the length of its body. Each of the three parts of	42	14	65
the fly's body is very highly developed. The head, a great portion of	56	19	70
which is covered by a set of compound eyes, contains sense organs and	70	23	74
parts used to obtain food. The middle section, or the thorax, holds	84	28	79
the muscles responsible for flying and for moving the fly's six legs.	98	33	84
The third part is the abdomen, which is used to produce offspring and	112	37	88
to process food. All of these parts work efficiently together and allow	126	42	93
the housefly to break down organic material and redistribute the ele-	140	47	98
ments, as well as to annoy the people around whom it flies.	152	51	102

PLANNING YOUR SAVINGS

	gwam 1'	3'
Before you begin to set aside money for future use, you must decide	14	5	57
just how much you will be able to save on a periodic basis. You should	28	9	61
then think carefully about how and when you will want to spend some of	42	14	66
your savings. For example, your goals may include buying a car, earn-	56	19	71
ing a college degree, and financing a house. Money saved for such aims	71	24	76
should be placed in savings accounts or in very safe investments from	85	28	80
which funds can be withdrawn quickly. Savings for retirement should be	99	33	85
placed in one or more of the numerous individual and company plans avail-	114	38	90
able. Separate retirement accounts reduce the temptation to spend this	128	43	95
money for other things. Finally, you should not make risky investments	142	47	99
until you have allowed for the realization of all your major goals.	156	52	104

gwam 1' | 1 | 2 | 3 | 4 | 5 | 6 | 7 | 8 | 9 | 10 | 11 | 12 | 13 | 14 |
    3' | | 1 | | 2 | | 3 | | 4 | | 5 |